One cannot help being moved by th emotional *writing of these young minds. I heartily recommend this as a read to help understand the dynamics of our youth.*

—Mayor Dave Earling, City of Edmonds

The amazing power of the written word is so clear in these stories. The reader's heart is opened to the struggles students have encountered, and the authors are empowered by the courage it takes to write and share their stories with others.

—Mary Kay Sneeringer, Edmonds Bookshop

By engaging in personal healing and giving voice to their trials, these students are reaching out to those who are quietly struggling to tell them they are no longer alone.

—Ian D. Cotton, Lynnwood City Council

These stories truly amplify the voices and heroism of Scriber Lake's incredible students. Year after year they are given the opportunity to become the storytellers, role models, and advocates they were meant to be.

—Natalie Walker, Executive Director,
Rain City Rock Camp for Girls

THIS IS A MOVEMENT

THIS IS A MOVEMENT

Owning our Stories, Writing our Endings

Compiled and edited by Marjie Bowker, Shalyn Ensz, and David Zwaschka

STEEP STAIRS
PRESS

For information, contact:

Steep Stairs Press
23200 100th Ave. W.
Edmonds, WA 98020
425-431-7270

www.steepstairspress.com

www.facebook.com/steepstairspress

ISBN: 978-0-9974724-1-7

Library of Congress Control Number:

Cover Design by José Pulido
www.pulido.co

Print book and eBook formatting by Hydra House
www.hydrahouse.com

Editing assistance by Chris Kratz

*Freedom begins the moment you realize
someone else has been writing your story
and it's time you took the pen from his hand
and started writing it yourself.*
—Bill Moyers

Books published by Steep Stairs Press:

We Are Absolutely Not Okay | 2012

You've Got It All Wrong | 2013

Behind Closed Doors | 2014

We Hope You Rise Up | 2015

I'm Finally Awake | 2016

This Is A Movement | 2017

I was inspired to write my story after reading Santino Dewyer's story "Broken Promises" (2015). I went through a similar situation with my dad. He was never there for me, either, and I couldn't imagine having to explain it to anyone. I respected that he could do that.

—Madison Aguliar, 2017

I was inspired to write my story after reading Brayan Hernandez's stories (2012, 2013). I realized he had gone through a lot and still had the courage to put everything out there.

—Santino Dewyer, 2015

If it wasn't for Shalyn's Ensz's story "They" (2016), I would still be hiding my story from everyone. Sometimes it only takes one person to get a lot of people talking.

—Nikolas Cook, 2017

When I read Alicia Verzola's story "Any Last Words?" (2016) I realized I'm not the only kid who has gone through losing a parent, and that it isn't something to hide or be ashamed of.

—Caleb Stine, 2017

When I started going to Scriber, I felt alone and wanted to hide my story, but after reading Jaycee Schrenk's story "Growing Appetite" (2015) I felt inspired and confident to write about my life. I wanted to not only forgive my mother, but also myself; actually, the writing process has given me so much more than that. When I heard that Caleb Stine was affected so deeply by my story, that made everything come full circle.

—Alicia Verzola, 2016

When I first started at Scriber I heard Daniel Cohen read part of his story "The Sound of Goodbye" (2016) during an assembly. The scene he read—about abuse by his step-mother—has stuck with me ever since. It gave me a wave of confidence to step out and share my own experience with the world.

—Kyra Wasbrekke, 2017

All of the writers from We Are Absolutely Not Okay *described the writing process and how it helped them. I wanted that, too.*

—Kelly Makaveli, 2012 and 2016

When I heard Sarah Jean's story "Thirteen" (2016) it reminded me of how my dad treated my mom and how abusive he was with her. It made me want to write my story, too.

—Jocelyn Chavez, 2017

TABLE OF CONTENTS

A NOTE BEFORE YOU READ

As you read these stories keep in mind that some events may be triggering for someone who has experienced the same trauma. Remember to monitor your emotions. If you find yourself unable to continue, take a break, talk to a trusted individual, or go on to the next story.

FOREWORD

SHALYN ENSZ

"*Writing is a socially acceptable form of schizophrenia.*" I placed this quote from E.L. Doctorow at the end of my story "They" in last year's book *I'm Finally Awake*. Writing has been just as important in shaping me as a person as my schizophrenic tendencies used to be. Now writing, not my condition, is the force shaping my future. When I first heard about the "Scriber books" while performing in our annual Seattle Public Theater production two years ago, I didn't hesitate to approach Marjie about my own experience with hallucinations and delusions. Even though I was new to the school and knew little about the program, I wanted to be the one to write that story. I wanted to start a conversation about these tendencies in youth and to break stereotypes about the disorder. I knew writing it would help piece together the events in my head and replace the jumbled collage of memories that existed.

It's important to keep in mind that these stories are not written by professional authors with experience in the field of storytelling. Many of us had never written more than mandatory English assignments. It's hard enough to tell a personal story. It's harder still to face past demons with honesty and style, but that's what we've all done. Fortunately, I love to write, and I think that makes me one of the lucky ones.

Experiencing the sense of growth and community that occurs when working through draft after draft as a group has inspired me to come back and take a leadership role in the program. I've gone to dozens of events and spoken about Steep Stairs Press and how we have healed ourselves and inspired each other. But it's impossible to convey how much of an impact it's had, even after saying it hundreds of times to thousands of people.

All of the Steep Stairs Press writers from the past six years know how important these conversations are, and how the writing process is a large step toward recovery and acceptance. One of the first things new students are asked when they come to Scriber, myself included when I came two years ago, is, "What's your story?" Everyone has one, but it takes extra courage to re-face it and share it with others. As a school we have come to the realization that these stories are ours to own, not others' to judge. Every student has been inspired by a story in the past. That's the Movement. It's like a Rube Goldberg machine, each spark of inspiration playing off another until an entirely new story is written. Our Movement is removing the stigma around talking about mental illness, abuse, and addiction.

I've experienced direct inspiration through editing this year. While reading Alesandra's story ("A Scale, a Mirror, and Those Indifferent Clocks") about having an eating disorder, I was struck by the first scene, even though it was my fifteenth time reading the draft. The emotions she conveys and her descriptions about her eating disorder forced me to face the fact I'd been subconsciously denying: I was going through the same thing without even realizing what it was until I had her story in front of me. I recognized the behavior and was able to stop it before it progressed. The Movement is still providing hope for me, just like it did two years ago.

WHEN SKIES ARE GREY

CALEB STINE

"No one in the last six years of this writing program cried more writing a story than Ali did," Marjie says. She's sitting on a stool in front of the classroom and Dave is sitting at a desk in front of her. Marjie and Dave have been co-teaching and publishing Scriber student stories in books for the past few years. It's the final day of our spring "mini-course" and fifteen of us have been working on our stories from 9 a.m. to 2 p.m. every day for a week. Today is our final day, and I'm nowhere close to being done with my story.

"It was very painful for Ali to revisit her mom's death," Marjie continues, "but she made the choice to face it and worked on it all year."

Mom's death.

The choice to face it.

My stomach sinks and tightens.

Last year's book, *I'm Finally Awake,* is in front of me, so I pick it up and turn to page twenty-five. Her story is called "Any Last Words?"

"Ali's story is a masterpiece. It combines all of the parts we've been working on together. Take note of how she paints the setting, characters and emotion, and how she builds the tension through the dialogue in the flashbacks," Marjie tells us.

I started to write about my own mom's death in Marjie's English class in the fall, but stopped when I had to dig deeper into the details. I didn't want to think about what I had been repressing for so long. I put the story aside for a couple of months until Marjie asked if I wanted to publish. I refer to Marjie and Dave as "surgeons" because it's like they cut open my head to extract information. But for some reason I want this operation to occur. I want to publish because I've never really talked about what happened and I know it's time to get it off my chest.

However, on Monday, I found myself once again experiencing the kind of anxiety that placed me on the verge of puking multiple times. I just haven't been able to go there.

I turn my attention to Ali's story. Her first flashback is about the last Christmas she spent with her mom—how her mom had been drinking at a family get-together. I've read this story before, but for some reason the words are jumping off the page today.

As we read, the memories of the last Christmas I spent with my mom four years ago come back with clarity.

✌✎

"Merry Christmas!"

I heard my grandpa's voice as I came running through the hallway into the living room. He was sitting on our brown couch drinking his coffee, watching the news. The pile of gifts under the tree looked bigger than the night before.

My mom wasn't there, even though she had told me she would be. I stared into space—my thousand-yard-stare—like I always did when I realized she was going to be late. It usually didn't bother me when she didn't follow through except on big days like Christmas. I had seen her the day before and I knew she was going to spend Christmas Eve with Joe, her boyfriend of three years.

My focus returned to the presents. "Can I open them?" I moved closer to the Christmas tree and, when my grandpa didn't respond, I repeated. "Can I open them?"

"Hold on, Buddy. We have to wait for your mom to get home," my grandpa sighed. He was sick of waiting for her.

My grandpa, mom and I had shared an apartment all twelve years of my life. My dad was in the area, but I never saw him. He and I would go long periods of time without talking, and then every few months when it was convenient for him, he would force me to go to his house for the weekend. So it was just the three of us.

My grandfather was a bartender at Applebee's, but he was also a painter and had turned our dining room into an art studio. He kept all of his paints and thousands of brushes on the dining room table with his easel next to it. He was a kind, gentle man who always wore khakis, white K Swiss tennis shoes and his hair in a military flat top. My mom was a stay-at-home mom and had always been present up until the day she met Joe. I had hated him from the beginning. He brought out the worst in her; every time she came home after being with him she wasn't herself. She had usually been drinking and taking too many of her Xanax. She would always pass out and the tone of her voice would change. She would slur words or mumble.

"How long until she gets home?" I asked.

"She just called. She said ten minutes. Would you like any breakfast? Something to drink? Some milk?"

"No, I'm not hungry. Thank you, though." I tried to hide my disappointment and sat down on the couch to wait.

My grandpa looked at me and smiled—a smile mixed with love and sorrow. Then he said, "Would you like to open one present before she gets home?"

I jumped off the couch. "Can I? Can I please?"

"Yeah, Buddy, go ahead," he said.

I chose the smallest one first, saving the best for last, and opened it to find the *Star Wars* Legos I had asked for.

"Thank you!"

I figured there was no point in opening the package to play with them when my mom would be home any minute, so I sat down on the couch again.

Why isn't she here?

Why can't she hurry up and get home?

She knows this is important to me.

Close to an hour went by when we finally heard the click of the front door unlocking. I perked up at the sound. My mom walked in wearing a black coat, blue jeans and black Converse tennis shoes, her normal attire. She was holding four wrapped gifts.

"Merry Christmas, Poo Bear!" she slurred.

"Hi, Mom. Merry Christmas," I replied. I felt sick.

She walked over, handed me the presents, and sat down on the couch without taking off her shoes and coat. After I opened the second gift, her head drooped down and she started to nod off.

Forty-five minutes later, she woke up and stood quickly.

"Okay, Dad," she said to my grandpa, "I'm gonna go back over to Joe's."

"Whatever, Tova," he responded, still staring straight ahead at the TV. He took a sip of his coffee.

"What?" she snapped, throwing her hands in the air, looking straight at my grandpa.

He turned from the TV and looked at her. "You aren't even going to spend Christmas with your son?"

"I came home and gave him what he wanted," she said, pointing in my direction.

"Okay, Tova, just go. Are you coming home tonight?"

"I'm not sure. Maybe." She headed to her room and I heard the sound of items being thrown into her purse.

Before leaving she came over to where I sat at the couch, leaned down and kissed me. "Goodbye, Caleb. I'll see you when I get home. I love you," she said.

"Okay, I'll see you when you get home. Love you too, Mom," I said as I slumped the back of my head against the couch, wishing she would *just stay*.

She walked out the door, slinging her purse over her shoulder.

❧

As we continue reading Ali's story, I realize the last time my consciousness touched these memories was when I heard "You Are My Sunshine" play one day during class a few months earlier.

"*You are my sunshine, my only sunshine/You make me happy when skies are grey.*"

My mom would sing these words to me every morning while she sat on the edge of my bed, gently shaking me. Waking up to her voice made every morning amazing. Her voice was so soothing to hear first thing that I usually fell back asleep. Whenever I hear this song or even think about it, I tear up. When that song came on in class I had to leave the room.

I feel like leaving the room now, too. But I stay where I am. I'm frozen by the thoughts of that Christmas and by the memory of the song.

We get to the part of the story where Ali gets a call from her dad telling her that her mom has died. She doesn't believe him. The news about my mom came when I was at school, and I didn't believe it, either

❧

I found myself staring off into space once again in my dull, grey eighth-grade classroom. I was surrounded by the chatter of my classmates and the ticking of the clock. I had always hated math, and I hated the teacher, too.

My grey-haired, looks-older-than-she-should, puke-green-sweater-wearing teacher was like Cheerios with no sugar.

The phone rang and the class stopped. My teacher picked it up and said, "Caleb, grab your stuff and head down to the office," with a stern voice. She always spoke with a stern voice, even when she was trying to be funny.

Confused, I picked up my mechanical pencil and math notebook off the desk and put it in my backpack. Then I headed toward the main office. *Did they find out about something I did? Did I say something to a teacher I shouldn't have?*

Earlier one of my friends from my apartment complex had texted me asking if I was okay. I had just shrugged it off, but now I was wondering what he meant.

I reached the main office and walked inside to see my dad standing there, signing me out. He seemed more hunched over than usual.

Why is he picking me up?

I started to worry about my great grandpa because my dad never picked me up early. *Maybe he's in the hospital*, I thought. As soon as we left the building I asked him, "Is it Grandpa?"

He looked straight at me and said, "It's your momma, Bubba."

I couldn't believe the words that came out of his mouth.

Mom?

I stood there and just looked at him, stunned. "Mom?"

All he could do was nod his head.

I asked him a second time. "Mom?"

When he started to cry, I managed to squeeze out one more "Mom?" before I began to lose control of my body.

I could tell my dad didn't know what to do by the way he grabbed me and walked me to his car. He guided me to the back seat where my grandma sat with teary eyes. I flopped into her arms. My asthma kicked in and, since

I had forgotten my inhaler at home, I was both crying and gasping for air.

By the time we arrived at the house I had stopped crying and could breathe again. I opened the door, felt my feet hit the pavement, and shuffled inside when the tears hit me again. I saw the tan walls, the entertainment center with the big Vizio TV, the brown couch, and the table with my grandpa's painting supplies. Everything looked the same as it did when I left in the morning, except that family from both sides—my uncles, my grandpas, grandmas, and some neighbors—stood there, greeting me with silence.

My grandma—my mom's mom—came over and wrapped me in her arms. All she or anyone else could could say was, "Caleb, I'm so sorry."

At that moment I realized it was true. The only thing different about the room was that my mom wasn't in it.

She was gone.

❧

"I hate you, I'm never coming home!" Ali tells her mom in the story.

This is the place I haven't been able to go in my writing, the part I've tried to avoid thinking about for four years. I didn't want to think about her smile, her green eyes, the way she woke me up, or her long, blonde hair. I blocked out her soft voice as it spoke "I love you" before I went to sleep. I didn't want to think about any part of her because it made me remember how I would never feel her embrace again.

You'll never know dear, how much I love you.

But what I really didn't want to think about was the night before she died—the last time I saw her. I didn't want to remember the last interaction we had, or the words I said to her.

But here they were, Ali's words. My words.

"Caleb, it's bedtime. Shut your door when you go to sleep," my mom told me. She and her friend were sitting on the couch, talking, and they must have wanted some privacy.

"No," I answered. I hated sleeping with my door closed. I felt like something was always watching me from the closet, and I hated the darkness. I would end up lying there for hours, unable to sleep. She knew I felt this way.

"Listen to me, I'm the parent."

"I don't care."

"Close your door, Caleb."

"I hate you!" I screamed as I ran into my room before my mom could respond.

This was the first time we had fought over the closed door, but we fought a few times a week over dumb kid stuff like getting off my Xbox and doing homework. The fights were never fierce, but always left me angry.

I slammed my door behind me, jumped into bed and stared into the darkness.

God, I hate her so much. Why is she my mom?

I hate you! I hate you! I hate you!

That phrase has played over in my head for years, just like it has for Ali.

By the end of her story, all of the repressed memories are flowing through me. I can't stop them. Something inside me has been unlocked.

I find Dave a few minutes after we finish reading.

"Hey," I tell him. "I think I'm going to change my story. Ali's brought back a lot of memories. I'm going to take out the part about my grandpa and focus it just on her."

Dave nods and says, "That sounds like a really good idea. Sounds like it had a big impact on you."

I think about the impact. I haven't been able to think about her without feeling sad or sick for four years.

I leave the room knowing I'm finally ready to write it.

Please don't take my sunshine away.

A Note from Caleb

Writing my story has helped me talk about my mom's death with a little more ease, and it has also helped me release many memories I tried to forget. It has helped me clear my mind and get some things off my chest. The week was frustrating because I watched everyone else writing about what had happened in their lives while I remained stuck. By the end, though, I realized I didn't need to repress those memories because even though they may make me sad and really hurt, they were also the happiest of my life. My advice to anyone going through this: You will get through whatever life throws at you, just give it time. When you're ready to face it, face it. I knew when I was ready and finally acted on it. I plan to graduate next year and eventually go to school to study game design.

RAP MUSIC MADE IT SEEM COOL

JOSÉ CARVEL

My body is stiff, my chest aching.

Why is this box not a pile of ashes? This generic moving box, which I assumed held nothing more than old books, contains nightmares. All I was doing was cleaning, and out of all the mess around me this box was the closest.

I didn't ask to remember any of this.

It feels like small worms are eating out my insides as my eyes rest on my old Nike sweater. Torn and used up, it's splayed across my journals—journals from my dealing days. I unzip it, my hands shaking as I notice the hand-stitched pockets. As I hold it close, the familiar smell of cigarettes and 100 Años Tequila fills my senses.

The song Marco used to put on blast in the warehouse by Mara Salvatrucha plays as the memories from two years ago wash over me. *"Cheers!! This goes for the bad guys! / A car passes by very slowly, it's police..."*

This was my life when I was thirteen. The song, this smell, this music. *Damn, the rap made it seem cool.* It reminds me of my father. I think of the night two lifetimes ago when I didn't know what it meant to *hold a piece.*

The rain was pounding down hard, stormy and grey. My body felt chilled as we walked through downtown Seattle, the wind piercing my skin. I looked up from the the dull sidewalk and saw my father in his black Nike zip-up, matching sweatpants, and shoes that had a streak of red—my favorite color.

"Come on, José. I'ma show you something cool." He tilted his head over in a smooth way.

"Okay, Papa."

I figured he was going to show me some cool graffiti. My dad loved art and he had taught me how to draw with all sorts of mediums.

When we made it to the overpass, homeless people littered the area underneath. One guy was slumped over a dumpster and another had a little fire going. Darkness surrounded us as my dad led me deeper into the overpass.

He stepped behind me and I felt a sharp pain when he grabbed a fistful of my hair.

"Be quiet," he said in his deep, gravelly voice.

What's happening? Why is he being so forceful? My mind was foggy, my insides scrambled. A body bumped me from ahead and I found myself staring at a buff chest. I looked up, thinking it was a homeless person.

"I'm sorry," I said, confused.

That was when I felt the first blow: a fist to my forehead coming from the white wife-beater in front of me. The hit was so powerful it made my whole body hurt, and I could feel the difference between his soft flesh and the hard metal of his ring. I stumbled back and saw more men, ranging in age from about seventeen to early twenties. Their voices were deep and they spoke in Spanish as they looked over me. One sounded very confused.

"¿Es éste el nuevo?" he asked.

"¿En serio?" another replied.

"Parece muy joven."

Why did my age matter?

Before I could open my mouth I felt an undercut to my gut come from beside me, knocking me back. The same man then balanced on his left foot, crouched, and swung his right foot into my shin. I thought my bone was going to crack from the impact.

I looked up at my father, who stood watching me. His face was content and he was nodding and grinning.

"Papá, ayúdame!" I cried out, my words muddled by saliva.

Why isn't he helping me?

As he looked at me crying for help his brown eyes seemed elated. "Shhh. . . Cállate, José, no llores, mi hijo," he said.

Why was he telling me not to cry?

Another shove came from nowhere. I fell to the ground and curled up on my back, fists floating above my face like a boxer block. They surrounded me and I felt harsh kicks, one after another. They pounded my body.

I bit through my lip and tasted metal to keep from crying.

One of them mounted my waist; he had a side shave with a star buzzed into it and wore a dirty white tank top adorned with two golden chains and a rosary. He tried to pry my arms from my face, but gave up and began to ram his balled-up fists onto my hands, making me hit myself. I glanced over at my dad.

He loves me, right? Why is he just standing there?

After what felt like an eternity, I watched as he raised his hand, still smiling.

"Eso es suficiente, levántate," he said, his voice smug and pleased.

I groaned. *What was enough?*

My father lowered his hand and held it out to me. I stared at it and after trying to figure out what he meant, I grabbed it and pulled myself to my feet. He looked at the men as they walked over to him. Their hands hit their chests and they made the infamous symbol I knew all too well: a sideways eight with two ones one each side, symbolizing an *18*.

I had known my dad was dealing drugs, but with this gesture I knew something more. I watched the news stories about shootouts and drug cartelling every morning while drinking milk coffee with my mom. I understood. My father was in Barrio 18, and this was my initiation.

My body felt numb as we walked back to the car together. I felt the fresh bruises growing on my sides. With a rough pull on my sleeve, my dad yanked me towards him.

"José, you are going to go through life wanting someone to share everything with," he said as my blood pumped. "But that won't happen. You are going to rot alone in a fuckin' hole. When you need someone it'll be only your family who will be there for you. If you betray us we will let you fall, and no one will ever be there like we are. You better get that through your skull."

I dug my nails into the flesh of my arm and began to scratch, which made a familiar warmth emanate from my chest—it was my way of coping. When I focused on the sting on my forearm it calmed my fast-beating heart. My father knew how I coped because we had been through a lot already. He knew this would leave more scars on my arms, but he didn't care.

I breathed out and looked down as we continued walking toward the car. I could see him out of my peripheral vision, watching me, enjoying the show. Heat welled in my eyes as tears streamed down my cheeks. He watched, stone cold, as I broke down.

Despite his speech about family I had never felt more distanced from them, or from everyone, as I did in that moment. I had just completely disassociated from myself. I was no longer me. I was truly alone.

❧

The lyrics of the song continue to fill the room. "*Gangs in my neighborhood run the corners...*"

I look down at my jacket and bite my lip, breaking the skin. I taste blood as I move the jacket to the side.

This pain is God punishing me for all of my sins.

I get up and lock the door to make sure my mother isn't anywhere near and sit down again to continue digging. I find my old journal and smell opium as I flip through my logs of drug deals and locations. My body feels *that* need, but I shake my head and go to the back of the journal.

I thought I had burned all this stuff. I didn't want evidence of that life for my mom to find. She had worked all through this time and didn't know about my involvement with the gang. She is the hardest working person I have ever seen and the last thing I wanted was for her to hate me. When the drug money started to roll in I would sneak out, sell heroin and other hard drugs, then drop twenty dollar bills into her purse when I got back. She was always so tired that she thought it was tip money.

I find my first cigarette butt and the date under it with a small note that reads: *It's so hard to breathe in so casually.* I had tried hard to make smoking look easy, like Marco and my dad, but it never worked. I coughed way too much.

✑✑✑

"¡Date prisa, pendejo!" Marco complained. He wanted me to hurry.

It had been two months since I took the beating called "my initiation" and we were going to the house of a client—this would be my first extortion. We were supposed to be protection for them but the money they had given us a day earlier wasn't complete. Recently their home had been caught in the middle of gang fights.

Marco was like my brother; he never laid a hand on me and always stuck up for me, even in front of my father. Marco looked scrawny, but when he got angry even my dad was scared of him. My dad had asked him to train me instead one of the other "punk-ass guys."

I rolled my eyes and hummed passively. I followed Marco as he walked up to the apartment made of chipped red construction bricks; the small windows made it look like a prison. He pushed me forward to the door and smirked.

"Ya gotta rough em' up a little. Ya feel me? Make 'em remember not to pull this shit again," he said with an amused look. I could smell the cologne we both wore, Curve Viva La Juicy Sport; he dressed me as a "mini-him."

I puffed out smoke—Newport Reds. My dad smoked these. "You want me to like...punch them?" I asked.

Marco groaned. "Bruto! No, no... Just push 'em around. Make 'em know that you're in charge."

I wasn't scared because I had lost my sense of fear at the initiation. Nothing could be as scary as that.

I nodded and pounded my fist on the dark, worn-out door. A man quickly peeked out from a crack. I noticed a tattoo of the name *Jennifer* in cursive wrapped around his forearm.

He looked uneasy when his eyes landed on mine. He sized me up, then glanced at Marco. He was no older than thirty. He had a buzz cut and was shaking in his black polo and coffee brown slacks. The way he shook reminded me of my little Chihuahua, Cupid, when he got cold or spooked.

"What do you want?" he whimpered. "We paid on time!"

I stared at him and shook my head. "Cállate, gringo," I hissed.

He stepped out of the doorway, showing himself fully in surrender. "Please understand, you raised the prices and I—" he wheezed, trying to breathe normally.

My fist rammed his stomach. I felt like a ghost watching the puppet that was my body move on its own. I grabbed him by his contorted features, placed my hand across his face, dug my thumb and forefinger into his temples, and threw him to the concrete sidewalk. He landed on his back and curled up. *Rough 'em up*, Marco had told me. I was doing just that. No longer would I bottle up my anger. All those times I was beaten and left on the floor writhing in agony during my month of training I hadn't been allowed to hit back. Now I would make this man feel that instead. The heat rose to my face so quickly it felt like it might bubble over and make me cry.

From the way Marco snickered I could tell he was amused that I had taken things to this extreme.

I crouched down and smiled at him. "You're really fucking annoying..."

I pushed my cigarette into his forehead, twisting it to ash it out. I wanted to hear the sweet sound of his suffering. I wanted to see him beg for death. I wanted to see him so helpless that he couldn't even fathom escape, just like my father had allowed to happen to me.

It was my turn.

The man hissed and groaned, his face convulsed in agony from the burn. Marco laughed and walked over, searching the man's wallet and taking whatever money he could find.

"Consider yourself paid off, puto," I sneered.

As the weeks progressed I became Marco's right hand. He wanted to see my inner animal come out. He wanted me to ruin those who wronged us—to ruin them beyond facial recognition. I ran my fists into people's bodies, curb-stomped faces, and cracked jaws until my clean white Nikes had crimson red spots and our victims choked on their own blood.

My head hurt, my heart pounded, and I held back vomit at first, but eventually I became desensitized to it. The anger, the sadness, the hatred—I had lost control. That animal did come out, and it grew like an insatiable hunger.

At times Marco had to pry me away and snap me back to reality. I was no longer the sweet person my mother had raised.

❦

I throw the journal across the floor.

My eyes gaze through the rest of the items in the box. Everything about this moment is too much for my psyche to bear. I move aside another journal and see it: a bullet, brand new. My very first bullseye was done with this bullet, into a sack of rice in the warehouse. I had become the target. I feel the tears well up, my body weak and unready, I want to throw up. The song plays in my head.

"Living with death without knowing when it's gonna hit you / Nothing shows in your history when you're living the crazy life."

Thinking about the moment I was shot makes my body ache.

❦

The night sky was ebony. No stars dared to shine upon our infamy. I was uncertain and nervous. I felt queasy. All I had ever done with other gangs was fight. For once I'd get to negotiate. I had clashed heads with a moron from a color gang in the back of my apartments and now here I was about to have a so-called pleasant chat with 13. Like cops and robbers, we weren't supposed to talk casually. But we needed guns. Our recent hook up was nothing more than lies. The bullets were blanks. An empty sound, so here we were buying from the same people we got into shoot outs with.

Marco walked with his usual confident stride, and I walked a couple feet behind him with eight more members of our gang. We were meeting at a ghetto car dealership in Everett—it was run-down with car parts scattered about. It looked like a junk yard. I laid my eyes on Marco's back, his black sweater soothed my anxious heart.

"Ándale! Come out!" Enrique said, wanting them to hurry. Enrique was the leader of the prostitution in our gang. He trained girls and brought in new ones. He had brown, spiky hair with sideburns and a five o'clock shadow. He wore a white shirt stained yellow from his pits and a gray zip up over top.

I stood a little behind Marco, my palms sweaty, as we watched more than fifteen guys from 13 step out from behind a building. Some emerged from behind cars. A couple of the bigger guys were holding crates.

My chest pounded.

Enrique then shouted "Piece!" as he rammed one of the guys back to get us time to get to cover.

Horror filled me at that word as I scrambled behind one of the crates. Against it leaned a busted up blue car door, the glass shattered.

"Out of my way!" Marco screamed, shoving me to the ground. I groaned. The loud cracking sound of shooting rang in my ears to the point that I felt like they would start bleeding.

Before I could pull myself into another spot, it happened. A horrendous pain filled me, and the world moved in slow motion as I fell back and landed with a thud.

What is this burning ache?

Julio ran over and pulled me up with great force, then shoved me behind a crate for cover. "Estúpido! You tryna get yourself killed?" he hissed. He was our so-called medic.

My vision went black.

I woke up in our warehouse—our headquarters in Edmonds. They must have carried me to the car and driven me here. Through my blurry vision I saw cheap, plastic chairs littered about and the large cargo boxes looming over us. I gazed at the bloody rags Julio had used covering the ground next to me. The sound of cars sloshing through water echoed in my ears. I whined as I felt the tight ropes around my wrists, put in place so I wouldn't pull away or squirm during the removal. My body ached. I could smell the sourness of old blood and the light scent of opium.

As I listened to Marco and Julio talk in the background, worry and pain rang through me. My body was slumped on a plastic chair, and I was aware that there was a bullet in my shoulder. Julio stood next me, his shirt bloody. He ripped off my once-blue shirt and looked at the wound, gritted his teeth, and swallowed hard. He pulled out his kit and grabbed a pair of rusty brown tweezers.

The extent of his medical training was how to blanket-stitch a wound.

He made sure the ropes were tight before he spread open the bullet hole, causing a sharp, stinging sensation to course through my body. I whimpered and tried to move, only causing more pain. The cold metal of the tweezers made my body spasm.

"Hijo de tu puta madre!" I screamed.

Marco ran over and gagged my mouth with his bloody tank top. I huffed and then calmed, hearing Julio's voice telling me not to sleep.

Another small metal piece of the bullet was taken out, and again a harsh pain shot through me, as if my arm was being torn apart. My body shook. I felt so cold. My teeth dug roughly into the cloth.

Julio slapped my face. "Tú vas a estar bien..."

I didn't feel I would ever be okay. I groaned and felt my body numbing. Julio continued slowly, removing all five pieces of metal.

When I finally felt my arm again, I was sweaty, feverish, and still bleeding. Julio walked away, then came back with a metal rod. He cleaned it and began to heat it with a torch lighter. I panicked and began to struggle.

"Shhh..." Marco cooed. "He needs to close the wound, paisa..."

I felt the burning metal being placed inside the bullet hole and my flesh sticking to the pipe. When he pulled it out, everything was foggy. I whined and let out tired, muffled screams. He pulled out a knife and heated it. When they folded my flesh over the wound I screamed and rocked the plastic chair.

Julio hissed and pulled back.

"Ah shut up, pussy." Then he began to wrap up my arm.

I awoke to the smell of opium hours later. My high was already set in because I had inhaled a fair amount of opium during my sleep. The other guys in the warehouse were hotboxing the entire place.

I realized the ropes had been cut, so I stood and looked around. The giddy high sensation made my pain feel like nothing,

Marco was laughing with some of the others.

I chuckled lightly and said, "Los dos son idiotas."

The heat of self-hatred fills me as I grit my teeth and shove everything back into the box.

I have to get rid of it.

The smell of my mother's fresh sopes fills me as I pick up the box, walk out the door and onto the cold street toward the dumpster. I open the lid, throw it in and hear it clank against metal. The putrid smell inside makes me feel more nauseous than I already am.

"Nunca más."

My head hurts. I need a smoke.

Every step I take back to my house feels heavier and heavier. I just want to melt into the ground. I don't deserve to have a home, to be with my mom. I hate keeping secrets from her. Someday, when we are both a little more mature, I will tell her everything. I will tell her that I was going behind her back to be just like my dad—her biggest fear. And I will feel so much relief when she knows. She's my best friend. She's worked so hard for me, and I feel I messed up everything in return. I can never express my gratefulness to her. But right now I can't afford to tell her the truth. She would reject me. She wouldn't even be able to look at me.

Back in my bedroom I lock the door once again. It's been almost two years since I wasn't allowed to cry. However, now my dad isn't around to force me not to.

A Note From José

After being shot I drowned myself in a drug addiction; I was high 24/7. Two months later, on October 3rd, I decided to get clean and leave the gang. After three days of locking myself in my cousin's bedroom to detox, I went back to the warehouse, confronted Marco, and haven't been back since. It meant a lot to me to be sober for my little sister's birthday not long after that, and I've been clean for almost two years now. I decided to write my story to show others that it can get better. Throughout the writing process, I've learned that it wasn't all my fault—that I may have done some bad things, but I'm not a bad guy. I still deal with self-hatred and the daily difficulty of confronting the person that I used to be, but counseling and the staff at Scriber Lake High School have helped me to reinvent myself. It's still hard to talk about my father; I have refused to have contact with him for now. I'm on track to graduate in a year and a half and plan to attend art school so I can become a tattoo artist. I'm also interested in culinary arts and fiction writing. Marjie wants me to become a public speaker, but I'm not sure how I feel about that yet. I have chosen to remain unknown. Like I mentioned at the end of my story, I'm not ready for my mother to know about my past. One day I'll confide in her, but for now I remain somewhat silent. I hope others will find comfort in my words. I'm now in the movement. . . maybe you will be, too.

A SCALE, A MIRROR, AND THOSE INDIFFERENT CLOCKS

ALESANDRA MARTIN

A harsh light flicking wakes me. A nurse steps through the sliding glass door, balancing a tray of food on her arms. I turn to look the other way as she places a steaming potato on the table next to me.

Nausea overtakes my senses.

Carbs, carbs, and more carbs. Others see something delicious, but all I feel is hatred for the potato.

"Sit up," she tells me. "I'm going to take your vitals."

Nurses arrive one after another like revolving doors. They all wear clean scrubs and blank faces. They bring food and then take away the tray untouched. They give supplements, medications, fluids, updates, and tests. They take my vitals every two hours.

I stare down at my baggy leggings, too big to fit properly anymore. My bones protrude from my hips, jutting out like sharp spears. My chest feels like a piano, every rib showing from the bottom of my ribcage all the way up to my neck. My hands encircle my thigh, inches away from my upper body. All of my joints ache. Having little to no body fat takes a toll on the way my bones interact. They creak and burn at times, whether I'm sitting or standing.

My love for such signs of malnutrition has become a sick, twisted pleasure.

My thoughts swirl with numbers—my weight and calorie counts. Along with the beeping of my heart monitor, they feel like my only company. I hear children screaming, babies crying, and parents trying to quiet them throughout the hospital. I wonder how I got here, how I came to be a skeleton wearing a hospital wristband as my full identity.

I was six when I first met Ana. I was confused and distraught. She followed my every step after this encounter, surrounding me with her voice, smooth as silk, drilling the rules of perfection in my head.

༄༅༅

We had been playing at my friend's house for a while, laughing so hard my jaw ached. We were both trying to jump higher than the other on her mother's lowly placed bed. We finally lay down, exhausted and out of breath.

After a moment she turned to me with a sparkle in her eye and asked, "How much do you weigh?"

I panicked. The tone of her voice was certain and final, like my weight was something I should know. Something very important.

I tried to act nonchalant, shrugging in fake indifference.

Her lean childlike figure pulled me into the bathroom, held my hand and pointed to the scale, signaling me to step onto it. I saw dissatisfaction on her face when she looked at my numbers, and I instantly knew something was wrong with them.

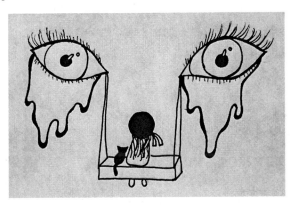

She stepped on after me and we both watched as the numbers went down. In her smile of superiority at her glowing numbers on the scale, my stomach fell into a pit of disgust.

From then on the bathroom was my church, my faith was the hope for smaller numbers, and my god was the scale. I would pray at night to the god my childhood placed on me, asking and begging to make me thinner, to have a pretty face, to just be. . . better.

∾

The potato sits next to me, untouched. I hate it so much.

I know my body is eating itself. The fat goes first, of course, and when I start to run out of fat, my muscles will be next. At night I feel my heart beating so slowly and so hard, I'm scared it might just stop. Sleep is a sanctuary for me during these times of exhaustion. If I'm asleep, I don't have to eat. If I don't eat, I sleep more. A beautiful cycle.

Just one more pound.

One more inch.

One more day.

One more trip to the toilet.

My mind is always clouded with food, body checking, counting calories and exercising, so I don't have time for emotions.

The most calories I let in are with alcohol. People question why that is, and I explain that just as my eating disorder gets rid of emotions and makes me feel better, so does alcohol.

Another nurse enters and takes the vital cuff from my arm. Shame radiates through me as she stands expectantly beside my bed. I can tell she is staring at my scars. I run my fingers along my forearm, touching them, the bumpy tissue marring my arms in purple gashes. I feel the raised tissue when I close my eyes; I have memorized each and every surface, each memory and reason for being there on my body.

I don't want my scars to define me. I don't want people to assume that my story is written in dead nerve endings. I think back to when I had the first desire to destroy my milky white skin.

❧

"Why don't you *love me*?" My mother stormed toward me and jabbed a violent finger into my ribs. "Have I not been a good mother?"

I stood my ground with raw fury and stiff muscles. I didn't know how to handle my mentally unstable mom. "You used to be."

Her face crumbled and she began to cry for the eighth or maybe ninth time that day. My sympathy for her had long passed. At the age of eleven all I could do was just stare at her with dead eyes and a cold heart full of hate.

She pushed me into the wall. Even though it was a light push it escalated through my unsteady body. She had never been violent with me before.

I stared as she fell, sobbing, into a heap of limbs on the floor.

"I'm sorry, Alice. I'm sorry..." she sobbed.

Her crying annoyed me so I walked to my room without glancing back. I sat on my bed and boiled over with anger. I didn't know how to react other than to slip into a coma of thoughtless hate. I never thought I would describe my mother as someone who slurred her speech in disconnection from a stable reality. That her eyes would wear purple bags like a fashion statement and her hands shake like an unstable Coca-Cola can.

Right after I stormed into my room, I heard a large crash and I knew instantly it was her. I *knew*, but was far too into my clouded hatred to check on her.

When my sister, Elizabeth, called for me, I went to the top of the staircase and saw her standing over my mother.

"I just want to die! I don't want to fucking be here anymore! I don't want to do this!" my mom cried. She continued to swear and pledge to kill herself.

My sister looked at me. "Go get the phone," she said.

"No! Don't call the police!" My mother gripped Elizabeth's leg and pleaded. "They'll take me away!"

I stood with the phone in my hands. I didn't want to go anywhere near her, but my sister continued calling for me to give her the phone. Finally I descended the stairs and got close enough to hand it to her, then turned and ran back to my room.

My mother cried into Elizabeth's ankle as she called the police.

A few minutes later the sirens showed up at my doorstep. There were two cop cars and an ambulance. They helped my mother up the stairs and onto our couch in the TV room, where she continued to cry. Her overreaction about her ankle made my cheeks burn in annoyance.

The police wanted to talk to us but I had nothing to say.

Elizabeth pulled me onto her lap, and with her arms around me the tears finally started to flow. I sobbed silently as she described what happened.

"Has she ever expressed wanting to die before?" one of the policemen asked, catching my attention.

She nodded. "She's said it to my father, and…" she paused, considering her words. "I see cuts on her arms a lot and I pull knives out of her room."

That was my first introduction to self-harm and the start of a new chapter in my life. A chapter that included my mom being away at Fairfax for two weeks.

≈≈

I try to shift in my bed to get more comfortable, but the thin mattress does little for my aching bones. The scratchy blanket does not protect me from the cold room, and my flat pillow does not make my head feel relaxed.

I go through the usual list of reasons I shouldn't eat the potato: the potential calories and the ton of weight I will gain.

The reasons not to eat it are stronger with each thought. Nothing can compare to the high of an empty stomach, to the power of refusing food while everyone else eats loads and loads of calories.

When people notice my weight loss, I'm in control. I'm strong because I can choose not to eat. Because I can go without food for days when no one else can. Because I can control my weight, I have so much more time than everyone else does. Meals don't slow me down.

I know my body is dying. I'm always cold and sleeping all the time. Climbing a single flight of stairs feels like running a marathon. Fainting is always a possibility.

Stand for too long? Faint.

Stand up too fast? Faint.

Get too anxious? Faint.

There's no stopping the black spots in my vision, no avoiding my knees buckling under my weight, no way to evade falling onto the floor in a heap of limbs.

I'm frustrated at how much I believe in my irrational thoughts. Minutes pass as I keep quiet, waiting for the nurse to leave me in peace.

I think about the complete turnaround from that time when I was eleven and how much I love my mother now. Her laugh is contagious and she is much more beautiful than she thinks. Despite her wanting to have her thirty-ninth birthday every year, her skin glows with an everlasting young spirit. I'm excited for her to visit me later; her company helps this dreary, empty room, and I know I can talk about mental health with her because she understands exactly what is happening with me. She continues to fight against it every day.

Another nurse enters and begins to type my numbers into the computer. Her attention turns to me and my uneaten meal. "You have to eat. Otherwise there will be consequences," she says, crossing her arms in an authoritative fashion, emphasizing the word *consequences*.

My eyes meet hers. I read the keypass she wears with her name: Alexis. "I know," I whisper.

I stare back at the potato. The steam has faded and is cooling down. I know my consequence will be a feeding tube, and I know how much it will hurt. It's a pain that burns every second, one that I remember from a few months ago.

❧

They gave me a big glass of water. At first I assumed I wouldn't drink it all, but once I started I gulped it down.

"First we're going to measure where the tube will end in your stomach," the nurse told me.

I had gotten the tube a year earlier. But I didn't remember much of it because I was too drugged. I remembered sitting in the chair with the arm rest. I remembered them taking the tube out of the sterile plastic. I remembered the tube going down my throat and them placing me into a wheelchair. Only flashes of images, then blackness.

They held the yellow tube up to my left side and made a Sharpie mark where my stomach ended. Last time they warned me and told me to relax before shoving it into my nose, but the nurse in charge didn't seem to care for such courtesies.

It burned. I couldn't comprehend that my nose was linked to my throat in that way.

"Drink the water. It'll help the tube go down easier," she said. I gulped and it went down, making me gag uncontrollably. The nurse rubbed my back. "Just give it a second, Sweetie."

I knew it was necessary. I had been admitted two days earlier for complications from malnutrition. They told me my body was shutting down, heart failing, body fat gone, and that my organs were next. Under normal circumstances I would have fought the admission by my mother, but my depression gripped me into a state of indifference.

With every swallow, every cough, every bite of food or drink of liquids or move of my throat, I felt the scratching of the tube.

The sanctuary of a hospital doesn't feel like a sanctuary if it's unwanted.

I had never wanted to die more. I had given up hope for my future, for my distant plans for my life... I didn't care anymore. I was in a limbo between physical life and emotional death.

༺༻

I think about the way I grew up noticing my body, my mother, and the feeding tube. I pick up my plastic fork and mull over my choices.

The logical state of mind pushes past the uncertainty in my thoughts and I put the fork in my mouth.

As I chew I feel defeated, guilty. The eating disorder in my head is screaming at me, like it always does. With every bite it's telling me what a failure I have become and that I shouldn't give in to the lies my logic gives me.

With the same bite I feel empowered by defying the voice in my head. Defying the unhealthy choices I've grown accustomed to.

The potato slips down my throat and I swallow. By my own choice.

A Note from Alice

I continue to fight my eating disorder. My recovery is far along, but I have so much further to go. Physically I have made it out of my unhealthy state, but mentally I´m balancing on a scale of demons. I read the stories of other peers in previous books and was inspired to share my story because I want others to understand what can go on in the head of someone with an eating disorder. I want to show that a meal is so much more to us than supplement for one´s body. Writing this down has helped me deal with my past and look towards my future. I aspire to be a nurse, to help touch the lives of those who are sick and to make their road to recovery easier as many nurses have done for me. I want to give back to the people who saved my life countless times, medically and emotionally. The title *This Is a Movement: Owning Our Stories, Writing Our Endings"* really shapes the basis of my writing: I'm still dealing with struggles in my life, but I'm changing things for myself. I will graduate early, stay healthy, and plan my long-lasting future...writing my own ending.

JUST ONE TOUCH

SHANIJA NESBITT

A hit on the side of my waist.
It was nothing.
Get over it.

But my heart is racing out of control.

I'm in my eighth grade English class, sitting next to my friend Eric. We had been whispering rather than doing our work and were trying hard not to laugh out loud because we knew Mr. Thomas would separate us. But Eric said something that made us both bust out laughing and had hit me on the side of my waist.

That is all that happened. Just a little tap from my friend.

But that one touch brings back the memories of that day, and suddenly the smell of the room is making me choke. All of the guys who didn't bother changing out of their gym clothes from first period mixed with the scent of Mr. Thomas' teacher-lounge-made coffee is making my head spin.

I stare off into space, trying to distract myself by counting the small plastic chickens scattered around the room and examining the old *Star Wars* and *Star Trek* posters.

But I flinch again and the uneasiness begins to wash over me. Just a light touch, but a touch in the spot where Jayden hugged me multiple times that day, just three months ago.

✥

"Those are some cute shorts," Jayden said as he twisted his short, dark curls.

He put his hands in his swim-short pockets and his slight, chubby cheeks formed a grin.

I looked at him and smiled.

Jayden was the neighbor of my nephew, Damarion, and he had come over to spend the night. I had been staying with my sister Shalonda at her house for the summer while my mom worked, and Jayden always hung out with us since Damarion was just about his only friend. Jay and I weren't that close and I never went out of my way to hang out with just him. He was mysterious and mature, and a lone wolf who seemed to know more about the world than we did. But I did consider him to be a friend. He always paid close attention to me when he came over, but I appreciated it a little bit more in that moment since mom and I had been getting into arguments lately.

"Thanks," I said with some confidence.

He continued to stare at me.

My sister called us into the living room to go out for lunch and Damarion left the room. I stood up and he walked closely behind me and put one arm around my neck and one around my waist, hugging me.

I thought of it as a friendly gesture, nothing more.

"You're so pretty..." he whispered, his breath on my neck. I was lost in his sweet, boyish scent and didn't want him to let go; it was the most attention and love I had gotten all week. He pressed closer and grasped my waist tighter, making my stomach churn and my side ache.

I figured my sister was probably about to come find out what was taking us so long and tried to pull away from his grip, but he held on even tighter.

I tugged some more. "Jay, move!" I said, finally releasing from his grip, flinching my shoulder back.

He scoffed and rolled his eyes. "I'm gonna go get some pizza," he said, annoyed, his nose slightly scrunched up. I stood at the bedroom door and watched him stride down the hallway as if nothing happened. I rubbed my side where he had held me and it was sore.

❧❧

"Wait, listen to this—" Eric says, starting another cheesy joke.

"Shanija, Eric, move to separate sides of the room, now!" Mr. Thomas yells. He could convince a lion to stand down with just the sound of his voice.

We jump up and make faces at each other. I sit in the corner of the room and my mind goes completely blank. I feel like I'm going crazy. That one single touch has made the memories of that day with Jay run wild in my head.

I see pictures of him flashing in my mind, and I think I'm going to be sick. I raise my hand to be excused from the suffocating classroom. Not even waiting for permission, I get up and leave.

❧❧

Damarion, Jayden and I headed to the garage to get in my sister's car.

"Shotgun!" Damarion called, making the heat rise up to my ears because that meant I had to ride in the back seat with Jay.

"Let me get the door for you," he said. He rushed over to the back door, his sandals flopping on the oil-stained ground, and held it open. I hesitated at first, unsure if he was going to hug me again.

He just likes you. Stop being such a brat, I told myself.

His tall body towered over me as I smiled at him and tried to sit down as quickly as possible, but he used his quick reflexes and squeezed my butt before walking over to the other side of the car. I sat down stiffly.

The only thing that moved were the shivers going down my spine.

My sister came down the garage stairs wearing her Tweety Bird shorts and a fuzzy black jacket and Jayden greeted her with a raspy laugh.

"Now, when we get inside the pizza place, don't act up, or y'all gonna end up eating nothing," she said firmly, flipping her straight black hair over her shoulder.

We all nodded in agreement as Jayden leaned closer and put his hand on my thigh. I tried pushing it away, but he tightened his grip. When I winced in pain he started to stroke it more softly and whispered, "Sorry."

Crossing my arms, clenching my teeth and squeezing my eyes closed, I occasionally switched my leg positioning to move his hand from time to time. Eventually I just let him continue because I knew I couldn't do anything to convince him to stop.

As soon as we pulled up to the pizza shop, I got out of the car first and rushed inside. "Yeah, can I get two pepperonis and one with sausage and pineapple?" I said to the girl at the counter.

Damarion walked in with one hand in his baggy shorts pocket and the other twisting the ends of his short afro. He touched the top of the door with the tips of his fingers. He was a foot taller than me, even though I was two years older.

"What are we ordering?" he asked. His dark skin and brown eyes almost glittered in the light. Smelling his familiar mix of baby lotion and heavy Playboy cologne was the only thing keeping me from going crazy.

Jayden gave everyone dirty looks as he followed us inside and stood next to me. When he was mad, he felt like he had to be mad at the whole world. I tried to concentrate on the cashier counting the money instead of the way he was looking down at me, but I could almost hear him roll his eyes for the millionth time.

As we moved over to wait for our food, I finally said, "You know, you don't have to do that."

"Do what?" he shrugged.

"Act like a child when things don't go your way."

Damarion came closer so he could listen to the argument.

"I don't know who you think you're talking to," Jayden said. "You're starting to be really annoying."

"You're starting to be really annoying," I repeated, mocking him. It was amusing to see his face scrunch up and turn slightly pale.

He got closer to my face and said, darkly, "Little girl, I'll rip every inch of you apart and eat you straight up just like that pineapple sausage pizza over there."

A cold feeling rushed over me, almost as if a blizzard had come through the door.

I had heard my sister talking on the phone with my mom about Jayden hitting his mom when his anger skyrocketed. Something as small as his sisters teasing him could trigger it, she had said. Damarion and I were terrified of him, but almost in a good way, like how in church everyone says you're supposed to "fear" God. But of course, we never let him or my sister actually *think* we were scared of him because that would have just made us look like a couple of babies. Plus, the one thing Jayden and I had in common was that we both had horrible anger problems too, so we cancelled each other out like two positive-charged magnets.

"Just keep talking smart. You'll see," he said, backing down. He gave me one hard last look and went to get the pizzas from the counter before heading back to the car where Shalonda was waiting.

Damarion watched Jay's exit with wide eyes and let out a breath of air. "Ooh," he said, snickering and twisting on his hair some more. He patted me on the shoulder and led me to the door. "He's kidding. He's just a weirdo."

"Yeah," I answered. But I knew that half of the things Jay did and said weren't jokes. I could tell he was serious and was trying to put me in my place by creeping me out. And it worked.

❧

I splash some water on my face, breathing in slowly, not even caring about my makeup running. If I had stayed in that room any longer, I would have puked.

The bell rings and it's time for math. I keep a wide distance from people, like a quarterback dodging anyone trying to tackle him. I don't want to think about Jayden anymore; he's already ruined my day without even being physically here.

In class I don't raise my hand eagerly like I usually do; instead I want to reach across the room and choke my teacher for talking about fractions while I'm breaking down in the middle of class. My senses are high and I don't even let my closest friends get near me.

When the bell rings I'm the first one out the door.

"Shanija!" my friends call after me. But I plug in my headphones, hoping they will get the hint.

I try my hardest to fall asleep that night, but I can't. The one memory I want to forget about comes back to replay in my mind.

❧

During lunch everyone sat in silence, and the air in the room was thick. Damarion and I exchanged a few tense looks. Jayden seemed to notice from time to time, but he didn't bother to speak up again. The rest of the day I didn't say much while they mostly talked about basketball. That night, we were all supposed to sleep in Damarion's messy room.

I always slept there when I came over; his dirty clothes, books, and video games were always scattered across the floor, making the room feel small enough without Jayden sleeping on a giant beanbag that took up at least half of the room. It was a warm, late June night, and our loud box fan hummed.

Jayden had been humming over it and picking at his fingernails for at least ten minutes before I finally said to him, "Jay, go to sleep."

He rolled over on his side and stared at me. "How?" he said. "You're lying right next to me."

I rested my head on my hand and just looked at him, frustrated.

He sighed. "I'm sorry about what I said at the pizza place," he said. "I hope you know I was just playing with you. I haven't been in the best mood lately."

I felt weird about him apologizing; usually he meant everything he said and that was it.

Does he think I'm actually buying this?

"Yeah, no I get it," I lied.

He smiled and I felt a slight warmth inside, glad that we had settled whatever had gone down hours before. Feeling more settled, I drifted off to sleep.

I woke feeling something crawling on my ankles and looked up to see Jayden at the bottom of my covers, making 'O' shapes on my ankles with his fingers, staring right into my soul. Even though it was dark and I couldn't see his eyes, I could feel them on me.

When I tried pushing him off he sucked his teeth, making a 'tsk' sound. My chest started to feel hot.

I turned from my side over on my back, feeling the cold air of the fan on my face. I pushed the covers back a little.

Then I felt a heavy weight on top of me. At first I thought it was Damarion falling off his bed, like he did when he got comfortable in his sleep.

But it was Jayden.

Again.

"I can't take this anymore," he whispered as he lifted himself up on both arms and looked straight at me, his face a few inches from mine.

"Take what?" I asked.

A jolt went through my body as he started pulling up my shirt. I became fully aware, my eyes bouncing around the room. After ripping my shirt from my body he started to pull on my shorts.

"Okay, Jayden, knock it off," I said shakily, pushing on his chest.

But he didn't stop.

My skin felt cold and my heart dropped.

"Jayden! I said *no!*" I whispered loudly. The air around me was suffocating. I looked over and saw Damarion watching wide-eyed from his bed. I gave him a hard glare, insisting that he stay down and let me handle it.

I kicked and pushed Jayden until he started to laugh, and then he pinned down my wrists, giving me no way to defend myself. My palms were sweating, but not enough to slip away from his grip. I was shaking uncontrollably and I couldn't breathe.

"Just let it happen," he said, his face so close to mine I could smell the minty toothpaste he used. He was using that damned smooth voice he used to get anything he wanted. But the one thing he wasn't going to get was me—I could promise that.

The light coming from the window showed that Jay's eyes weren't a chocolate brown anymore—they were pitch black. But there was something else: I knew he was enjoying the fact that he was the one in charge, and that I was no longer talking smack to him

I wanted to reach up and choke him. I wanted to cry and scream. My wrists were stinging, my eyes foggy and watering. But I knew Jayden fed off of fear like a demon, so I had to show him I meant business. With all of the strength I had, I kicked him in the stomach just as Damarion was getting up, about to take action.

Jayden grunted and held the area where I kicked him.

"Go to sleep, now!" my sister yelled from her bedroom, annoyed by all of the noise we were making.

I quickly jumped up in nothing but my bra and shorts.

My nephew flopped back down on the bed and sighed, relieved that the scene was over.

Jayden had gotten his dose of rush for the night. He smirked and shook his head and laid back down on the bean-bag like nothing had happened.

I watched him fall asleep, my heart pounding. Finally, I got my things and went to lie down on the living room couch, where my thoughts started to run wild.

How did a little attention turn into this?

What did I do for him to do this to me?

It's my fault. Why in the world did I wear those shorts?

Did he hear me say "No"?

Yes, I know he did. He did . . . right?

I let this happen. I could have easily seen this coming.

I swallowed the lump I was holding in my throat and a shiver went down my spine.

I wake up around 4:00 in the morning, covered in sweat from my nightmare, and let out a shriek. My mom comes in from the next room, looking confused.

"Why are you screaming?" she asks.

"I just had a bad dream," I answer quickly. I can't tell her the truth.

It happened months ago.

It's irrelevant.

It shouldn't matter anymore.

I sit up in the dark and stare at the corner of the room where I imagine Jayden standing. Even though he moved about a year ago without a trace, he is still with me. I just hope he isn't here to stay forever.

A Note from Shanija

This summer, it'll be three years since Jay attacked me. He didn't come back over for a while after that night because of a fight between my sister and his mom, and eventually, he moved. I was very paranoid and had nightmares for a year and some months, and I hated it when anyone, even friends or close family, touched me ANYWHERE. I struggled throughout middle school because of the pain Jay caused, and falling behind in school built up more stress. I wanted to write this story to help me finally tell my mom and sister what happened that night, since Damarion and I never spoke about it again. There are a lot of boys and girls who get raped, molested, or sexually assaulted and don't speak up about it because it's hard to bring up or they're afraid no one will believe them. But I hope my story will help people realize they aren't alone. I thought I was, and ended up building up my feelings and bottling all of them in my head for two years. But I finally realized it wasn't my fault and told some of my closest friends, who didn't judge me. I had a hard time forgiving Jayden, so when I typed out all of this on paper, it felt like I finally took charge of my story and was no longer a victim. I felt like a survivor who had finally written the end of that chapter of my life and started a new one, even though I went through emotional stress re-living it. I'm a freshman this year, and I've earned all A's and a 3.8 GPA and I might have a chance at graduating early, so I plan to work even harder. I definitely want to go to college, but I also want to put some time into my music career. Rapping is something I've wanted to do since I was seven.

WHEN THE STORM FIRST ENTERED ME

JAYDEN GREEN

My father pulls a cigarette from his pack of Newports and sparks it. "You don't smoke these, do you?" he asks.

It's the winter break of my junior year and he and I are taking a walk on his final night of a week-long stay. The sky is blanketed in dark clouds, and the sidewalks are only slightly illuminated by streetlights.

"No, I don't do that kind of stuff," I lie.

"Good," he replies. "I don't want you to get into this shit."

Actually, at the age of sixteen, my mind has been rewired by chemicals to the point that I no longer enjoy normal activities sober. But I don't want my dad to know this; he and my grandparents would be so disappointed. This is exactly what they have always feared for me.

We stop at a short white gate a few blocks from my house.

"Don't ever let anyone get you into drugs," he says. The sound of Akon playing from his phone in the background feels unfitting to the seriousness of our conversation, but the branches of the weeping willow, which look like dead worms hanging from tree bark, fit perfectly. "Trust me, I've seen where that stuff leads you. You don't want to end up like me, do you?"

I don't want to meet his eyes so I look down at his mud-covered boots and baggy jeans.

No, I don't want to end up like him.

My head feels heavy. I know he's trying to look out for me, and even though his life had crossed into a void from which he can't return, he's always tried his best to keep me from ending up the same way. Secretly, though, I've followed the same dead-end road.

"No, I don't," I say, trying to sound normal.

I had begun my descent from reality through abusing cold medicine just six months earlier, at the end of my sophomore year. I loved having my head in the clouds, feeling so numb and out of touch with everything. I no longer wanted to exist within this world.

But my best friend, Andrew, who had been sober from it for the past year, had given me a wake-up call during a recent Teen Night at the Lynnwood Bowl and Skate. I had stopped using, but I was still trying to figure it all out.

❧

"Dude, look at your face," Andrew said, cringing. "It's all yellow. You look gross, man."

"What do you mean? What's wrong with my face?" I asked.

I was holding up my head by my arms, which rested on the red, rectangular table. I was too spaced out to be aware of my surroundings other than the loud, shitty pop music playing in the background.

"Just go to the bathroom and look at yourself," he said.

I stood and rushed over to the bathroom on my rented inline skates. When I looked in the mirror, the person looking back at me appeared to be nothing more than a rotten corpse of what was once a teenage boy. The pigmentation of my skin had changed to yellow; my eyes were outlined in dark circles, my cheeks flushed.

I skated back to the booth. "Dude, what happened to me? Why do I look like this?" I said, hoping for a different answer than the one I knew was coming.

"It's the cough medicine," Andrew said, leaning closer to me for effect. "Do you not realize what it's doing to you? You're so spacy all the time, and it's like you're not even really there."

I wanted to deny it, but I knew he was right.

"I didn't know it could be this bad, man," I said. "I don't want to be like this."

"Yeah, that shit's evil, dude," he answered with authority. "People don't realize it at first, but this is what it does to you. Now, please, just promise me you'll get off that stuff, man. You're my best friend, and I don't want to see you do this to yourself."

My mind fired with depressed thoughts. I was leading myself down a thorn-covered pathway I believed I would never walk as a child.

I've failed the child I've tried to hold inside of me.

I've failed my family.

I've failed the people who have desperately tried to steer me away from this lifestyle.

Andrew and I left the skate rink, emerging from the flock of people all crowding by the doors awaiting their parents' arrivals. The cold wind brushed against my skin and I felt relief breathing the freshness of the outside air. We stood with our backs against the railing by the skate rink doors, our bodies propped underneath the blackened sky.

I'm a walking chemical waste dump.

I'm a skull filled with a blank space from where I rocketed myself into this black hole.

My head is now a living room where white noise can slumber away, like a static-filled television set.

Andrew's mom pulled up. He got in the car and I waved goodbye to both of them.

As I walked towards my grandfather's truck I decided that I didn't want to be that person.

I opened the truck and hopped in. My grandfather greeted me by asking, "Did you and Andrew have fun?"

"Yeah, we did."

My dad and I are silent as we walk to the house.

When we get inside I lack the energy to do much. Even though I haven't used since the night at the skating rink, I feel awful.

I lay on my bed and listen to "Absolution" by Sadistik, drowning myself from the outside world. I lay in my thoughts, picturing my dad, seeing how his life has turned out and what it must be like to live that way, to be unable to raise a son due to your own mistakes.

Not long after my parents divorced when I was two years old, my father became homeless and addicted to drugs, so it was impossible for him to raise me. My mother, along with many other problems, had been evicted, so I went to live with my grandparents. I had never really been close to either of my parents, especially my mother, who would disappear from my life for years at a time. I had hoped she would just magically return ever since I was nine years old.

If my mom was here right now, what would she think of me? Would she be proud to see what her son has become? Maybe it's best that she's gone, at least for now. I'm glad she doesn't have to know what kind of person I've grown up to be.

I think about the last time I talked to her, two years earlier.

I was sitting by the fountain outside of the Edmonds Starbucks when my phone rang with an unfamiliar number. When I answered I heard a deep female voice on the other end.

"Hey, Jayden. Do you know who this is?"

"No," I replied.

"It's your mother," the shaky voice said.

Her words sent me into an off-axis bubble of bliss; my stomach felt like a knot tied in multiple directions as my brain was being pulled apart. It had been five years since I last heard from her.

"Oh, hey," I replied. I got up and started pacing back and forth on the sidewalk.

"What have you been up to?" she asked, trying to sound confident. She seemed unprepared, like she didn't know what to say. At least we had that in common.

"Nothing much, just trying to keep up with school work and stuff," I replied. I stopped pacing and stood still.

"What grade are you in now?" she asked.

"Ninth."

"Oh, so you're in high school?" Her voice became louder. "How old are you?"

A cloud of sadness hovered over me. *How could my own mother not even know how old I am?*

"Fourteen," I said, trying to sound as if nothing was wrong. Then she started to ask simple questions like "Do you have a girlfriend yet?" and "How are your grandparents doing?"

I tried to picture her as we talked. I thought back to when I last saw her and wondered if she still had brown curly hair that matched her eyes.

"Hey, I have to go," she said. "I'll call you back in ten minutes, alright? I love you."

My head pounded like a heavy bass. My insides rushed as if my heart was racing down a highway of worried thoughts and false hope. I didn't want to lose her again, but I had to face reality. It would have hurt too much if I didn't.

"Love you too, Mom," I said. We both hung up.

She never called back.

❧

I stare at my popcorn ceiling and let the words of Sadistik float through my head.

Right now I don't want to wake up or try to forget when the storm first entered me/Lately I've felt self destructive/Self-inflicted, self help the cuts with/ Shell shocked, hell's bells and trumpets/Self-taught to tell tales in public of this life, same shit but different day/I write it down, same shit in different ways/ Fight it now, break fists against the cage until I climb on that slave ship and drift away.

The lyrics intertwine with my life and raise my awareness as I listen. I've become self- destructive, a slave to the chemicals that created the mental wounds I inflicted upon myself.

I don't want to drift away on the slave ship.

I'll break my fists against the cage and do whatever it takes to escape.

I want to forget when this storm first entered me.

I drift asleep to the music with a peaceful thought: hope that this is the start to a new chapter in my life.

A Note from Jayden

Since that October at the skate rink and the talk with my dad, I've realized where this kind of life could potentially lead me—a place I don't wish to see myself in the future. Even though my drug use didn't end there, I no longer enjoy the feeling of being out of my mind and have hope that I can leave that part of my life completely behind. Currently my father has a home in Everett and I see him every few months. I've heard from my mother a couple times recently, but I still await her return into my life. I hope that my story will give others courage to acknowledge their need for change. It's better to live life how it was meant to be lived rather than surrounding yourself with self-destruction, whether it be to escape from something or just out of curiosity. Writing this has helped me reflect on my past self and notice the positive changes in my life. Nowadays I keep myself busy with friends and writing rather than letting myself slip down the rabbit hole. After I graduate I plan to go to college to take classes in music production and writing, as those are my two favorite hobbies.

"We're all born into this river without knowing how to swim, and eventually we learn how to keep this water under our chins." —Eyedea

YOU OF ALL PEOPLE

CRUZ GARCIA

When I get the text I grab a sweater and my hat, walk out into the rain, and climb into the packed white Charger with five others. All six of us are wearing white t-shirts with Lucky's picture on the front.

I'm still drunk from last night's bottle, which makes everything seem even more fuzzy. We start driving to the cemetery in silence while King Lil G is bumping. On the way we stop at Safeway to buy some flowers to put on the casket. There are three police cars observing the funeral grounds—one out on the road and two inside. Rumors were circulating that the rival gang was coming to shoot it up, so Lucky's family asked the cops to come and watch.

We turn onto a gravel road with tombstones on each side, take a left, and see a lot of cars and about fifty people standing under a green metal cover that is protecting the casket. We pull up behind some cars and walk up to where everybody is standing. When we see the gray casket I feel anger at its beauty. Lucky was a graffiti writer and told us he wanted us to tag our names on his casket when he passed away. But this one was too nice; no one asked us to tag it.

What happened at the party plays in my head again and again; I feel like it will play like this for the rest of my life. There is so much I want to say to my best friend.

I wish I could trade places with you, Lucky. It's my fault 'cuz you were kickin' it with us that night. You knew we were gang members and that the rivals haunted us, but you didn't care. You were down for us. Somebody should have gone out with you when you went outside. You shouldn't have gone alone. It shouldn't have been you. You of all people. I want to cry every time I think about it. It hurts, man, finding you like that. Damn, Homie, it breaks my heart.

✎✎✎

I was sitting next to Lucky on the couch at around three a.m. The mixture of drunkenness and high off of the dabs had made the carne asada they barbecued in the backyard taste so good. It was a cold night in December and we had been partying for the past five hours. We were drinking, smoking, and playing card games. . . having hella fun.

Lucky had Snapchat open and kept trying to take pictures of all of us while we covered our faces. Lucky was always messing around, always having fun and laughing. He was a really good dancer and artist and was known for walking around saying, "These hoes ain't loyal," because one girl had broken his heart. He was wearing Rico's black hat with the Steelers logo, which he had borrowed and never given back.

It was a normal night, nothing out of the ordinary.

We had been friends for four years, best friends for the past year. It was always Leo, Lucky, and me hanging out on Casino Road. Lucky's mom was dying of cancer and his dad was in the drug scene. My mom was on heroin and my dad had been deported four years earlier. I lived with my aunt, but she didn't care what I did. So it was just the three of us hanging out. We always had a good time.

My homies went out to the garage to do more dabs. Lucky went with them, but I was already too tired and high so I stayed on the couch.

I was drinking a Modelo when I heard "*PA PA PA!*" It sounded like a cap gun, but I knew it was gunshots because I'd been shot at plenty of times before. I got up and ran to the door and opened it cautiously. My heart was beating like a drum. It was very quiet outside except for the music bumping in the garage and the only light came from the glare of the street lights. The cold winter air gave me goosebumps as I walked toward the garage. When I opened the door, smoke and the smell of beer and cigarettes hit me.

"Hey! Did you guys hear those gunshots?" I yelled over the loud music.

Rico looked up, confused. "What gunshots? You're trippin', Drowsy. There wasn't no gunshots."

I looked towards the street and saw something on the ground.

"What is that?" I said and pointed towards the front of the black Escalade. I walked over to see what it was and I realized it was Lucky. He was slumped over on his knees and Rico's Steelers hat was on the cement in front of him.

As I pulled him up he made a sound in his throat trying to gasp for air. He was struggling to breathe.

"Lucky, Lucky, wake up!" I yelled. But he was unresponsive.

My homies came out of the garage. "What happened?"

"I told you I heard gunshots," I said, shaking. My heart felt like it was being stabbed.

"He probably just hit his head on the front of the car," one of them said.

"We have to take him to the hospital," said another. Two of us tried lifting him but we couldn't; he was so heavy he felt like a pile of bricks. My other homies started to help. It took six of us to finally get him in the car. We put him in the back seat, slumped over so he was lying on his shoulder. I got inside and sat next to him, feeling confused and hurt. I saw blood coming from his face and blood all over the back seat. I was so hurt and broken.

I said, "Fuck this! I can't do this," and left the car.

I sat down on the ground and buried my head in my knees as they drove off.

"Fuck the rivals! I'ma kill them motherfuckers!" I yelled as tears fell down my face.

❧

I can't walk up to the casket because it hurts too bad. I stand in the back with a few others for a while, then kneel down, look away, and cry.

Even though I'm here, I'm not really here. I know his family is saying words in his memory, but I'm not comprehending much. I'm thinking about that night, going over and over it in my head. I had been up for three days straight following Lucky's death and have slept only on and off since.

"He wasn't part of the gang. He was a good kid. He didn't deserve this," Lucky's father says as he cries. "We just lost another family member."

Lucky's mother had died a few months earlier. Right after her death Lucky and I sat outside on the stairs of our friends' apartment building at night and talked about our families. He talked a lot about her that night... how much he missed her and how he needed to do better for himself. He had moved in with his cousin, but he didn't feel wanted there. He told us he was going to always kick it with us so he wouldn't have to be home very much.

I miss kicking it with you every day and talking to you. I could tell you anything and everything and you would always back me up. I'm so happy I got to get close to someone like you. It was hella filthy always posting on the block with you, Homie.

Lucky's brother comes up to us after his dad stops speaking. The night Lucky died he and I held each other and cried through the pain.

"My family wants time just for us," he says. "We're going to put her ashes in with him."

"Okay," I say. I start walking back to the car, but I don't want to leave him yet. I know they wouldn't ask me to leave if I was here alone. They know I was Lucky's best friend.

We walk back to the car. The mood lightens and everyone starts to joke around. I try to join, but my heart isn't in it.

I miss you so much. I wish it was all just a dream, that one day I will wake up and find out that shit never happened. That you are fine and doing good. I can't wait to see you again, Homie. You were my best friend, my motherfucking brother. I will never forget all those fine memories that we shared. I know one day I'll see you again and you will be right there waiting for me with a smile on your face.

A Note from Cruz

I started drinking heavily after Lucky's death. I drifted away from everybody and stopped going out altogether for a couple of months because I was in a deep depression. Despite all the partying, I started doing well in school when my living situation became more stable. I started to feel more positive about myself and my future. I decided to write this story because I felt like I needed to get it out of my mind. It was very therapeutic to write because I was able to release a lot of the stress I've had for the past year and half. I've been doing a little better than before—I even have a job now. Because of the people who took me in, as well as the support I have at school, I've been showing up to classes more often so I can graduate next year. I'm trying to get away from all the negative people in my life. My future dreams are to become the best father I can be so my children will never experience the things I did, and to become a psychologist. I want to be something big in life so when I die people will remember the good I've done instead of the bad. Here's a message to readers who are going through a struggle: Always keep your head up and live life to the fullest. Life is what you make it, Homie. Don't follow the wrong road, because one day you're going to realize that there's more to life than just a block and your homies. Remember the people that will bring you up in life instead of pulling you down. But if you fall down, get back up.

DIRT POOR AND A LITTLE HIGH

AKASIA TRAYNOR

I can't believe I'm actually here, in person with him, my birth dad. It's been a couple months since I moved in with him, but I still love looking over and seeing him drive his bulky white truck, one hand on the steering wheel and a nasty clump of chewing tobacco in his gums. I'm more aware of the air entering and leaving my lungs when I realize I'm finally living with him again after fourteen years. It's overwhelming in the warmest of ways, especially when it's a simple Seattle spring day like today—the best kind of day to stare out a car window.

The bright colors of trees, road signs, and abnormalities catch my eye as I sit in a little moving box with the person I can't possibly get enough time with. I barely know my dad, Beau, but I feel connected to him. I think it helps that he's on the younger side, with a naturally tan complexion and rays of rosey red faded onto his cheeks. We have the same smile, people say. I think they mean the shape because his lips are thinner than mine, and his teeth more yellow and crooked from years of drug use. A quiet scent of cigarette smoke still follows him wherever he goes, but he doesn't have that strung-out look anymore, like I imagine he did during his prime time of jail visits and grimy living.

He playfully hits my shoulder while rapping to Tech N9ne's song "Red Nose," which is blasting out of the stereo. It's crazy how I'm suddenly sixteen and with him, smelling the same quiet but cozy, dusty-house smell of his car and holding real conversations. My chest has a slight aching feeling with how content my heart is.

I remember this same feeling from a couple years back when I first met him. I try not to think about it too much because I know how dangerous it is for me to get lost in thought and I really don't want to ruin the moment. But it's hard not to. I was thirteen when we went to a little gas station to pick up snacks and he was singing "Sweet Child of Mine" by Guns-n-Roses. He looked at me with that same goofy grin we share and lightly hit my shoulder, trying to bring me into the now—just like he does almost every car ride.

I try to distract myself from my overactive thoughts by lightly kicking one of the numerous empty water bottles scattered on the car floor. His cup holders are full of chew containers, empty wrappers, and tons of coins. That's not even the worst part—the back seats are terrible. They're piled with his dirty construction and gym clothes, plastic bags, shoes, and empty food containers.

I don't want my mind to wander away from the mess surrounding me, away from the present, to the walls my mind puts up to help me forget my traumas. I can feel my eyes getting heavy as I think about my mom. I met her a year before meeting my dad, when I was twelve. Maybe I can think about it a little bit before my dad drops me off at my boyfriend's house. That was a good day with her, so maybe nothing bad will come up.

I ignore the uneasiness in my stomach and close my eyes, allowing my mind to wander over those mental walls—to really visualize the tattoo on her collarbones.

My adoptive mom had driven me to a Starbucks in Seattle to meet her that day. I remember a lightning bolt of anxiety shooting through my body, leaving my legs weak as I glanced into the café. I stared at all the unknown faces wondering which one could be her, but I couldn't get to every face before opening the door. I felt like the world around me was moving in slow motion, even the air. I couldn't possibly get enough air into my lungs. I must have been hyperventilating.

Then I saw her. I knew it was her the second our eyes met, and I would have known it even if she hadn't gotten up to walk straight to me. Suddenly her arms were around me.

"Hi, Akasia. It's me, Sarah. I love you so much," she choked out behind tears.

I was shocked by how similar our eyes were. If pictures of just our eyes were laid out next to each other, no one could tell whose were whose— other than the freckle on mine. Hers reminded me of a forest; they were a calming green with wisps of yellow sticking out around her pupils, like whiskers. On that day they stood out even more due to the blue eyeshadow that matched her M&M-blue blouse. The long, delicate chain hanging around her neck held a silver, detailed heart at the end, which contrasted nicely with the blue.

"Hey..." I stuttered.

Her eyes shyly focused between me, the table, and her pile of stuff. "I brought pictures of our family and you as a baby. I also brought a journal we can pass back and forth between our visits."

I could hear her talking, but my mind wandered off again. We sat down, coffee in hand, my voice shaking with anxiety at every word I tried to say. When I looked at my mom's smile I saw an unknown but beautiful soul sitting next to me, the warmth of her heart bringing me in. She has a warmth that my dad definitely shares.

I look over to see the dragon tattoo on my dad's right arm, leading to his chest. I've always been interested in it, and even though it's faded now, I can still see the shades of a giant red and black cross in the middle. You can tell he works out just by looking at him. It's funny, though, because while confidence emanates from his wide, exaggerated gestures and easy-going strut, he's the kind of guy who not only asks everyone in the house if his shirt looks stupid, but he still changes it five times before leaving.

My mind clicks into the present with a more recent memory. A couple months ago while I was living in the Youth Care shelter, we were on one of our daily outings. We drove down a narrow Seattle street lined with short, steep driveways leading up to little, old houses. I swore one of the houses we drove by was my mom's because I remembered it from when I first met her and got to spend the night sometimes. But the windows were all boarded, so I didn't know for sure.

A reborn curiosity saturates my brain with a slight headache, so I finally yell over the music. "Hey, Dad?"

His arm leaves the middle console to turn down the volume.

"Yeah?"

I feel kind of weird asking the question because we didn't really talk about my mom often, but I blurt it out anyways. "Are the windows at my mom's house boarded up?"

"What?" I can hear the shock in his voice. "Oh, yeah. She hasn't punched through windows in a long while, but she's not doing good with her drug relapse. She does that when she's mad."

I can feel the muscles in my face tense; I mean, I already knew she had relapsed. That's the whole reason we've barely talked for the last two years. Still, it makes my heart drop. I decide to leave the conversation at that and turn up the music again. Right now I want to think about her when she was doing well.

My mind works its way back to sitting next to her at Starbucks. The tables were made of slick granite. I remember that because I noticed how the shades of marbled browns, greys, and slight pinks looked against the rings my mom wore on seven of her fingers.

She had started flipping through a big blue photo album. It was intricate and I smiled when I saw all the psychedelic doodles next to the pictures. She pointed at a few pictures of an old beer bottle with a signed letter inside. "It's cheesy, but this is the bottle we put in the Puget Sound on your eighth birthday." She explained how every year she, my baby siblings I had never known about, and a few other people would have a special celebration to remember me and wish me good luck wherever I was in the world.

In that moment, anger rushed through the depths of my stomach and rested in the back and sides of my head, burning at my temples. I wanted to clench on to her every word like a baby's fist wrapped around a finger, but all I could think about was that cold night I was taken from her eleven years earlier.

I hated CPS for taking me away from her. I was angry for what I missed out on.

I try to pay attention to how the dotted white lines turn to a solid white stripe on the road—anything to focus me back into the car with my dad. I can feel my face starting to get red but I can't stop my thoughts from going there.

I don't even know what I'd say to CPS if I had the chance to tell them how my life went after they took me away. I'm sure they wouldn't want to hear about the homelessness, abuse, and ER visits anyway. Maybe it's not my place to get mad, because maybe it wasn't their intention. Maybe it was just a job to them, following protocol. Maybe I was just another kid on a checklist. Maybe each one of them justified their decision by going home to their families, sitting down at dinner and talking about their new case and how irresponsible the parents were. Maybe they imagined the good home they would put me in and felt satisfied with themselves for having a "better," more privileged life.

But all I know is it destroyed me. It left me with my mind aching and spinning with questions upon questions.

What if I wasn't taken away from my parents?

Why didn't they want me?

For years I felt unwanted and lost in a world of "Who am I?" Then I met my roots and realized they weren't even in that bad of a place; they were just dirt poor and a little high. I would have had a way better life with my parents rather than the life they blindly chose for me. Sometimes I still get caught up wondering what my life would have turned into if I hadn't been adopted. If I hadn't run into the people I did, or experienced the traumas this life brought me.

But I have to stop these thoughts.

I feel a warmth spread on my shoulder and I realize it's my dad's hand, this time out of worry. "Are you okay?" he asks in a caring, but not-too-vulnerable way.

My face quickly forms a smile and I look at him, nodding. "Yeah, Dad. I'm fine."

He puts the car in park and I realize we are already at my boyfriend's house. I quickly try to get my stuff together, but I can see a worried look slightly creased onto his forehead out of the corner of my eye.

"I love you, Punky," he says.

I jump down from the truck and try to focus on the different-colored pebbles forming the pavement that leads up to the front door. I'm trying to get my mind into the right place, but I realize I forgot to say "I love you, too," before my dad drove away.

Walking up to the door is always kind of a blur for me. It's the few seconds where I get to prepare myself, which is weird because there's nothing bad ahead of me. In fact, it's everything good. The first healthy relationship I've ever had—and I've had a lot of crappy ones.

Focusing my breath back to a normal rate, I knock. As I wait I'm deciding whether I'm going to go for a hug or his cat first, but I know the third thing I will go for: his two heavenly warm blankets.

Skylar's beautiful blue eyes greet me. "Hi, Babe," he says, closing the door behind me. "I have to do chores real quick. It shouldn't take me very long."

"Okay, I love you. I'll be in your room."

Fifteen minutes later, Skylar walks in and sees me cocooned in his blankets. "Why am I not surprised?" he says with his slightly crooked, teasing smirk. I laugh a little, but he knows something's wrong.

"Are you okay?" he asks, lying on his side, facing me. My eyes flicker between the perfect little gap between his two front teeth, the red stubble that speckles his chin and above his lip, and the bright silver shine of his diamond earrings. I don't think he realizes how much I adore every little thing about him, but right now I'm just trying to avoid his eyes. I wish I could tell him how I want my mom and dad to know me better. I know exactly what I'd say if I could open up to him.

I'd tell him how I wish I could show my parents my heartbreak, my runny face, and how my scars were made. How I want them to understand my uneven brows, broken down fingernails, and self hate. I want them to smell the scent of freshly-made pancakes bounce off the colorful walls of a home turned upside down, to hear the laughter silenced in eerie halls of "what happened."

But I also want to bring them to the now, to who I am in the moment, the me without ghosts haunting my actions and fogging my brain. I'd bring them to my forest, to my getaway trail with broken bridges and mossy paths. To the serenity of shady ponds and the reflection of trees glimmering across the surface. I'd teach them that it's okay to be a tree-hugger, then they'd know me.

My dad would probably laugh and say I'm just like my mom. Or maybe he'd accuse me of being on acid. But at least he'd know me.

I wish I could say these things to Skylar, too. But instead I let out a silent, unconvincing, "Nothing." I try to look really distracted and interested in something as I focus my attention on his bookcase full of empty vape-juice containers and nerdy plushies. Now I'm trying to avoid looking at him all together.

I know he doesn't like it when I don't tell him what's wrong, but I can't help it. I really hate not being able to let out my feelings face-to-face, but I get scared of being so vulnerable. Nothing good has come my way from being vulnerable. Needless to say, my feelings come out one way or another.

All I want to do is bury my face in his chest because my entire body is shaking in a signal that "an episode is coming."

He holds my face.

"Are you okay?" he asks again. I can hear the confusion in his voice.

I start to space out and can feel my eyes slightly hazing over in blurry disassociation. I don't know what I'm seeing. Is it real? Is it whatever's going on in my mind? Are the hallucinations coming back? I have no idea, and I'm losing the energy to decipher the difference.

"Just PTSD again, babe. Don't worry, I'm fine. How are you?" I finally say.

But I feel a tugging sensation inside my chest as if it's trying to pull me down and away from the scent of his room. My arms shake and my body twitches as if hands are grabbing me then violently letting go. I don't know whose hands they are, but I can see my fingers move across my wrists in a scratching motion leaving behind long, red marks, and I can make out Skylar's hand coming to hold mine, stopping me from self-destruction.

For only a moment I feel grounded. Then I feel the panic shooting back through my veins up to a lump in my throat, and everything goes dark. I've fallen. My entire body feels heavy as I relive what happened. I can feel the cold drops of water falling on my skin and I have no idea if it's the rain from the night I got taken from my family or if it's my own tears in the moment. Subconsciously, I know I need to get away. It can't be real. *How can't it be real?*

It feels real. It feels like the officer's hands are around my two year-old body, lifting me from the cement and then peeling my fingers away from grasping my mom. I feel the evening air slice across my skin as he tugs me, my pudgy toddler arms frantically grabbing for anything I could possibly get my hands on. I shudder at the final image of the car door loosely slamming behind me, and the sudden silence that drowns out my mom's screaming.

But it can't be happening. I was just cuddled up in Skylar's bed, and I know my body isn't two years old anymore. And I know this suffocating feeling comes from these bad flashbacks. I know the screaming that's echoing through my mind isn't entering my ears.

It's all hallucinations. I know it is, but at the same time, I don't.

I clench my fists around Skylar's new sheets and try to feel the silky fabric between my fingers and brushing against my inner arm. I feel ashamed. I can feel the adrenaline leaving through my pores and my body feeling lighter...except for the overwhelming bucket of shame emptying out into my chest.

I don't like it when Skylar sees me like this. I don't want to be a burden. He assures me I'm not, though. I think he can see I'm slowly getting through the worst of the breakdown.

I finally bring my face out from stuffed in his mattress and look him straight in the eye. Tears sting my face, but I don't care.

Skylar brings me into his warm embrace and his words drift through my ears. "Let's dance," he says.

A Note From Akasia

I've been living with my birth dad and his lovely wife Oona for a few months now, and as long as things go well, my adoptive mom will allow me to live with them again next year. This has made a huge impact on my well-being, and while I still struggle with bad flashbacks, hallucinations, and other disorders, I feel a lot more grounded and safe. My birth mom is still going through a relapse, but we text every now and then and I love her with all my heart. I visit my adoptive mom often and appreciate all she has done for me. As for my boyfriend, he's a big part of my life and I'm extremely thankful for his understanding and patience, and for surrounding me with a healthy, strong relationship. I have many stories to tell, but decided to begin by writing about how adoption has affected me; eventually, I hope to safely access more traumatizing memories as a result of starting here. Writing through some of my hatred for CPS and PTSD breakdowns has helped me find some closure. Writing this story has also allowed me to express things to my parents and boyfriend that I haven't been able to open up about. Adoption is normal, yet also really confusing and mind-altering. If you are going through this, it's important to know it's not your fault. Nothing is wrong with you. You are not unwanted, unloved, or unworthy. You are strong, and I hope reading through my experiences will give you a sense of that. I also think it's important for people who haven't gone through adoption to understand how hard it can be. I hope to use my past to help others by graduating from Scriber next year, continuing to write, traveling for a bit, and eventually becoming a counselor for teens.

ARE YOU SOMEONE WHO BREAKS PROMISES?

JESUS ARTEAGA

"They're gonna send me to jail," I say to my mom as she and my little brother, Dylan, walk beside me into Denney Juvenile Justice Center. My mom is strict, and she's unhappy about my court date—my second one in a year for missing school—but she sucks her teeth and lets out one of her quick laughs at my teasing.

"They're gonna put me away," I add, pushing her.

I feel bad that she has to come here with me after what my older brother has already put her through, and because of all she's been through with my little brother's health issues.

She holds Dylan's hand protectively as we open the doors and are greeted by a security guard—an older woman.

"Put all of your personal belongings in here," the guard says, pointing at the bin. Then she looks down at Dylan, smiles and says, "Hi, Little Guy!"

Dylan smiles shyly and looks away. Every time I look at him my heart melts a little. He's lucky to be alive since he was born with a double aortic arch and underwent three open-heart surgeries before the age of three. He could've died at birth. I would do anything for him.

We sit on the bench to wait for my assigned attorney. Dylan grabs my mom's phone to entertain himself. We are the only three in the room, so it's quiet except for the opening and closing doors and the clicking of a keyboard from the front desk. I think about how much community service they're going to give me, but then I try not to think about that because it makes me more nervous. I cross my arms to stop myself from shaking.

When a door opens behind us I turn to see five guys, between eighteen and twenty-five years old, enter with their feet chained together. Four of them wear orange jumpsuits and one wears a black and white striped one. They stand still for a moment until an officer appears, then they follow him awkwardly across the room towards the other door.

I wonder what they did.

I think about my older brother who spent time at Denney. He was sixteen at that time, and was in for starting gang fights at Edmonds-Woodway High School. When I visited him here with my mom I was only eleven, and I remember him wearing a grey crew neck. They didn't make juvenile offenders wear the jumpsuits.

When he got out a few weeks later, I overheard a conversation between him and my mom. I could tell there was pain in her voice and it made me sad. I was too young to understand, but I knew my brother was a member of a gang and that my mother didn't like that. I thought I was going to have to grow up and be the way he was because he was always hitting me and saying, "You need to be stronger." I knew that he meant that I was going to have to fight someday, like he did. But when his son was born, he turned his life around and I stopped thinking I would have to grow up to be a gangster.

For thirty minutes we wait as other teenagers join us in the waiting room. Finally, a Hispanic woman wearing a dark grey suit walks through the door and sits next to me. She introduces herself as my appointed lawyer and then looks over some notes.

"Alright. So you've missed over twenty classes and you're only a ninth grader," she says as she starts taking notes on her clipboard.

"Yes. I've been missing a lot of school because I've been sick," I lie. Actually, I had been skipping school to help my mom take care of my nephew while she takes care of my little brother. But I don't tell that to my attorney because I had been told that legally someone else had to help my mom because I was supposed to be in school. But my mom had no help and no money to spare for a babysitter.

I can feel my heart pacing faster, distracting me from thinking about what I'm going to tell her next. I have it all organized. Then she says the words I've been expecting to hear.

"I see here that you've been missing a lot of school, but what is this? It looks like you've been skipping class."

My eyes keep going back to the clipboard. I can't stop staring at it, even though I can't see what's written there. I don't appreciate her condescending tone. "I was behind in that class so I just decided to chill at the school library to catch up on work in other classes," I reply with another lie.

The truth is I had been on my way to fourth period one day when my friend stopped me.

I knew he was a bad influence; he wanted me to skip and smoke weed with him. Although I knew the consequences of getting caught up with that, he seemed like my only escape from fourth period. The first day of class I had been assigned to a group table and I felt like they didn't really want me there. So I had sunk self-consciously into my chair and isolated myself. Eventually I just stopped going to class and went to the library to either sleep or daydream.

She continues to write with her well-designed, fancy pen, then looks up at me with one eyebrow raised like she is in deep thought.

"Last time you were here you made a promise that you wouldn't come back," she says. "When we get inside that courtroom he's going to ask you if you're a man who keeps his promises."

I sit back in my seat and shift uncomfortably. I had made a promise and forgot all about it.

Am I a man who keeps his promises?

I look up at the dim lights of the ceiling, then down at the carpeted floor. My mom is waiting for my attorney to interpret our conversation.

Dylan leans against my mom's arm, looking tired. I don't like thinking about my own character while I'm looking at him.

I remember the day after he was born. I saw him sleeping right after his surgery. He looked extremely comfortable, lying there with his little fohawk, but when I looked at his chest—cut open and exposed—all I could think was *damn*.

Whenever I see him looking tired now, after he's been running and jumping around, it hits me. His lips turn purple. All I do is worry that he's going to collapse or have a seizure. He had a seizure once but my brother and I were in Yakima when it happened, and my mom called to tell us about it, scaring us both. When he gets sick it hits him hard. One time we had to take him to the E.R. because he wasn't responding to anything. He was alive, still breathing, just not responding.

I want to be someone he can look up to.

Am I a man who keeps his promises?

My attorney finishes her notes and tells me she will see me in the courtroom. After a few minutes, my mom, brother and I follow everyone else inside, head to the back corner, sit on the benches, and wait. There are more people in the courtroom than I expected—around fifteen. My stomach feels empty. Not hungry. Just empty.

The judge, who sits at a big desk in the front of the room, seems like a judge you'd see on T.V.: black robe, old, and a big bald spot. Before long he begins calling up kids one by one, talking loudly because of how far away he is from everybody.

I can't stop rubbing my sweaty hands together, and my leg is bouncing faster and faster as I wait for my turn. I look at my little brother and the question I can't get out of my head keeps repeating itself in my head.

Am I a man who keeps his promises? I'm supposed to be his role model and look where I am now.

My friends and I knew "middle school didn't matter." But now I'm beginning to realize that all of it matters.

"Jesus Arteaga!" the judge shouts at last.

I walk to the front and sit in the open seat next to my attorney, who sits at the big, curved table in front of the judge next to two other attorneys. I don't bother to look at the people behind me. I can already hear in my head what they are thinking: *Look at this delinquent. Just like the rest of them. He's nothing but trouble.*

My head hangs down and my elbows press against my knees.

He shuffles his papers and pulls out my student information. He clears his throat. "You've been missing a lot of school, huh?" he says as he looks up from the paperwork, using the same condescending tone as my attorney. I look to her as if she is going to answer for me. But no, the judge continues to look dead at me.

I am too nervous to respond, but I know I am the only one who can. "Yessir," I answer, looking up at the podium.

Am I a man who keeps his promises?

I try to keep myself calm. I rub my hands together and feel the moisture. I have to think positively. I drag my hands on my pants under the table.

"But what's this? You've been skipping your fourth period?" he asks. He's no longer glaring at me; he now wears a disappointed, fatherly look.

I feel a sharp pain because I don't know how to react to that look. I haven't had my father around since the fifth grade. If he had been there for me and my family, maybe all of this wouldn't have happened, and I wouldn't be in court right now. If I can go through life on my own for this long, I can keep going on without him.

Suddenly I feel itchy all over. My face becomes flushed red. I know this feeling. Guilt. I keep thinking to myself, *Why did you do what you did? Why couldn't you just keep steady attendance? Look at where you are now.*

Are you a man who keeps his promises?

I look over my shoulder and glance at Dylan, curled up next to my mom. He looks confused.

Maybe my first step is to show him that he can look up to me. If I can show him I can graduate, then he'll be able to, too.

I've retreated into my own little world, but I answer the judge just in time. "Yes, only because I was way too behind on work in that class. I talked to my counselor about switching out, but they didn't let me," I say as I bounce my foot.

"Uh huh. So last time you came here you made a promise that you wouldn't come back. Are you a man who keeps his promises?" he asks.

"Yes!"

I am offended at the question, but I realize I'm even more offended because he had to ask it at all. I know I've been wrong; I've lied once again, but this time it's different. I can't escape it. The judge knows I'm lying since I *did* break my promise of not coming back to this court.

Minutes fly by, but it feels like I will be stuck here forever. He writes on my records while talking with the lawyers. I think more about my little brother and how I want to be a role model for him. And I think about what kind of role model my older brother has been for me.

Finally, the judge says, "All right. Since it is your second time here, you're going to have to serve community service hours. You broke the law. You will be doing a minimum of fifteen hours at an after-school program. If you don't complete this by October 7th, additional hours will be added to your time. Do I make myself *clear*?" He looks up and stares directly at me.

I've never had community service hours; the only time I've heard about that was back in middle school when one of my friends had it for possession of brass knuckles. I don't know what to feel, how to react, or if I need to speak up or not. So I just smile at him and nod, tip my head back and stare at the high ceiling. *Thank god.*

"Alright, Jesus Arteaga. Fifteen hours of community service due by the seventh of October. I just don't get what a bright kid like you is doing here."

My smile drops. His words repeat in my head.

What is a bright kid like me doing here?

A Note from Jesus

Those questions stayed in the back of my head for about a year until I enrolled at Scriber Lake High School last spring. Before that my life seemed cloudy and I just let life control me; I believed that "whatever happens, happens." But now I have a better mindset and my path is clear. School is going great for me; I strive for success and let nothing get in my way. My future goal is to become a psychologist because I'm interested in learning how the mind works and what motivates people's words and actions. I decided to write this story because something as small as skipping school could have had such a negative impact on my life and my future, and I'm so grateful that this experience opened my eyes and helped me turn that around. My advice: own your story, own the events that happen and don't let them control you. If you don't know what you want in life, take time to think about it and talk with someone: a friend, parent, or a teacher. Think about the things you enjoy doing and find a career in that. Do everything in your power to clear the clouds away, because life is extremely tough if you don't know what you are doing or what you want for your future. Now I'm doing everything I can to be a man who keeps my promises, and I only make promises I know I can keep.

SHE'LL FORGET LATER

MADISON AGUILAR

"**J**ust get out!" my mom yells. Her anger drops from her mouth and sits heavy on my chest like an anchor. "Run away!"

Her face is bright red from the five drinks she's already consumed. "You're just dru—"

"Goooooooooooo!" she screams, as if she's yelling with her last breath, her throat vibrating as she gets to the end of the long word.

Blood rushes to my cheeks and my nose tingles, letting me know that my eyes are about to start watering.

We're in the back yard surrounded by everyone who has been hanging out at our house all summer. My older brother, Marco, and his three friends stare at me with blank expressions, and my friend Ashley stands behind me with her hand on my shoulder, digging her long nails in to remind me she's still here.

Apologize to me, I think to myself. I don't hear other mothers talking to their kids this way, and I don't want my friends to think this is how our relationship is. Plus, she's embarrassing me in front of my crush, Trevor, who is sixteen; I'm only twelve, and I want to seem older.

I feel tears building under my pupils, so I turn away before anyone can see them drop—especially Trevor—and head toward the house. I'm mad at her for going too far and not knowing when to stop, mad about how out of hand she's gotten with her alcohol, mad that it's been only two months since she took her first drink at the beginning of the summer, and it's already come to this.

✌✰✩

My sister, brother, aunt, mom and I sat side by side on the couch. As I pulled "Little Red Riding Hood" out of the baseball cap for our game of charades, I watched my Aunt Kaylee get up, pour herself some orange juice and hit it with some vodka. I shrugged it off and turned back to the couch to continue.

I stuck my arm out, palm down, and my sister yelled, "Little!"

"Little Red Riding Hood!" my brother shouted before I could even act out the second word.

Aunt Kaylee came back to the couch with two tall glasses and sat on the right arm of the couch, next to my mom.

Two glasses?

I slipped into my brother's spot on the couch as he stood for his turn. I looked at my mom, then leaned over my sister's lap and held my mom's long, blonde hair out of the way to smell her drink. The familiar scent of cigarettes and Chanel perfume hit me first, but then I leaned further into the cup.

"Alcohol?" I said.

I knew my aunt had convinced my mom to drive her around to bars lately, or to get alcohol and drink with her back at our house a few times. I also knew it was none of my business; she was an adult. But I never liked the idea of her drinking. My dad used to drink all the time when he was still living with us. It was normal for him to take a shot of tequila and chase it with a cut lime and salt or a cold Corona. I was never able to tell when he'd had one too many because he wouldn't throw up, speak nonsense, or suffer from hangovers. I just didn't like the way people looked when they drank, and I didn't want to see my mom doing that, too. When I was six years old I made my mom pinky promise that she wouldn't drink, even though she never had before.

"What about that pinky promise you made?" I asked, lifting my brows and smiling to make it light.

"Oh my Goooood, Madison," she said. She crossed her legs and looked back to Marco, who glared at me because I was taking attention away from his turn.

My mom doesn't drink, I kept thinking to myself. *Why is she doing this? Maybe it's only a one-time thing.*

After that night, it was fun for a while. When my mom was drunk, it was a party. My brothers had their friends over, and Ashley, who lived just a couple blocks down from me, would stay over almost every night. We built bonfires in the backyard and my brothers turned our shed into a hookah lounge. We would have up to twelve kids over almost every day, and everyone had red cheeks—either from the hot sun or from all the running and smiling. My mom would sit on the back patio with her drink, cracking jokes with everyone and singing to our music. I loved her to death, so it felt nice to spend all day with her.

For years my mom had just locked herself in her room because of depression and pill use, so it made me feel almost like a normal kid to be able to hang out with her. But after a few weeks the alcohol that warmed her stomach made her heart cold and angry. It got to a point where it was never a good time when mom had a drink.

I walk through the house and out the front door and don't bother to shut it behind me. My heart sinks.

I'm so fucking tired of this.

I run my fingers through my hair, pull on my scalp and look up to the sky.. "I'm done!" I scream. My voice is raspy and I'm trying to breathe in between sobs. "*Mom!*"

It's like I'm trying to call out to the mom I used to have. The mom I miss so much. The one who was never in a drunken stupor.

❧❧

"Get out of my way! Get off!" my mom shouted and slurred in frustration while whipping her thick, ratted hair out of her face. Anyone walking past our large living room window would have had a clear view of us, face to face, toe to toe, fighting over her keys like an aggressive game of tug-of-war. She was using all of her body weight to make me let go of her. Ashley was next to me, watching with wide eyes.

"Please stop, Mom!" I screamed as my voice cracked into a sob. "No, you're not driving. You can barely walk!"

Aunt Kaylee had stopped coming around when my mom stopped being a fun drunk. And it wasn't the kids having fun and mom watching anymore, it was mom having too much fun and the kids making sure she didn't do anything stupid. I didn't know what my mom was doing. She was always acting like a teenager. I didn't know what her goals were.

She always drank vodka. No beer or wine. It was always the same drink. Coke with vodka.

Coke with vodka.

Coke with vodka.

We started to fight a lot. As the drinking got heavier, our fights got worse. I was lashing out and being disrespectful. Why would I want to be nice to her when she was drunk? I knew that after a couple more drinks I would be cleaning her puke and listening to her cry about how much she hated her life or how much she loved it. There was never an in-between.

My thoughts throughout the day weren't fun. *Is she going to be a happy drunk or a sad drunk? Is she going to want to drive to get more?*

My teeth clenched and both of my hands were on my mom's forearm. She finally relaxed, and when I relaxed in response, she snatched her arm free of my hands, stumbled back and went for the door. My adrenaline shot through the roof; my whole body felt like it was vibrating.

"Fuck!" I yelled, then looked at Ashley. "Door!"

Ashley looked stunned, her bright blue eyes filled with adrenaline.

"I'm fine!" my mom said as she stumbled toward the door. It looked as if her limbs were too much for her to carry, like there was a brick tied to the end of her arms and legs and she was trying to walk through water.

She shoved past Ashley and made it through the door. She ran to her red Jeep, got in, locked the door and turned the key. Ashley and I ran after her and pounded on the hood.

"Stop!" I screamed, trying to get her inner sober self to hear me. "You're going to kill yourself!"

"Janene! Janene!" Ashley yelled.

But my mom put the car in reverse, looked behind her and pulled away from us. We ran to the end of the driveway and Ashley jumped in front of her. As my mom put the Jeep in drive, Ashley hopped sideways, out of her path.

This isn't my mom.

My mom wouldn't do this.

I loved her, but all I could think about was how hard I wanted to slam her onto the ground, dig my nails into her wrist and hold her there. I wanted to scream in her face and tell her how much it hurt. I wanted to scream at her until my throat was dry and hard. I wanted to scream at her until her face was covered in shame and spit.

❧

"Maddie!" Ashley says as she follows behind me, trying to offer comfort.

"I'm done with her. She tried to punch me in the fucking face!"

"Are you ok? That's not her, she's just drunk."

It was better when she would stay in her room and watch movies all day. At least then she wasn't calling her twelve year-old daughter a slut and a bitch.

Ashley moves toward me and puts a hand on my shoulder, making me feel a little better. But her company brings my defenses down further. I cry louder and start choking on the air that I've been inhaling too quickly.

I thought my mom would have stopped drinking by now.

Why won't she change her life?

I thought my mom hit rock bottom the day she tried to kill herself.

⁓

I heard logs hitting the cement ground outside. My brother had locked my mom in her room no less than ten minutes earlier for throwing things around the house, and the pile of wood I heard falling was stacked underneath my mom's window.

I ran from my bedroom to the back sliding door and saw her, barefoot and wearing a red silk sundress, trying to catch her balance after landing on the stack of wood from her jump.

"Are you kidding me?" I said as I watched her throw an extension cord over an exposed board that was used to hold up our patio.

I felt the blood draining from my face as hot anger gave way to pale shock and horror. It felt like the corners of my mouth had magnets pulling them down. I finally gave into a full pout and let the water works go.

At twelve years old I get to watch my mom attempt to hang herself.

My heart felt charged by a lightning bolt, and adrenaline made the tips of my fingers tingle.

I knew she was having a hard time, but I had no clue she was capable of trying to kill herself in the backyard while her children were home.

I made my way over to her and yanked down the extension cord. My face was sore and tight, hot and drenched in tears.

But she was giggling. She reeked of alcohol, cigarettes, barf and body odor. She had bags under her eyes.

Why? What's so funny about this? Does she not feel anything seeing me stand in front of her like this?

"What are you doing?! *Why*?" I gasped for breath in between sobs. "If you kill yourself that will be it for me! Where would I go? I have no one but you!" The lump in my throat was sore. She straightened up and her face relaxed.

Then she started crying with me.

She looked to the back door. I knew she was waiting for one of my brothers to come out because she saw them more as fathers when she was drinking—the ones who told her enough was enough. My brother appeared in the doorway. His neck tensed when he saw her. He threw his hands in the air.

"Mom! How did she get out?" he demanded.

"Window. She tried to hang herself." I crossed my arms as I walked inside. I went to my room and plopped on my bed.

They can deal with her.

That isn't my mom. She's just drunk. She just needs sleep.

I lean against the Jeep to hide from my mom.

I scoop my legs closer to my chest and try to pace my breathing. Ashley puts her arm around me to get me to stop banging the back of my head against the bumper.

"It's gonna be okay," she says. Although I appreciate her effort, these words mean nothing to me. That's what everybody says when they don't know what to say.

"Do I just stay out here? Does she really want me to run away?" I say out loud to no one.

"Let's just go for a walk," Ashley says. "She'll forget later." She stands up and offers me her hand. I accept and let her pull me to my feet.

The sad thing is I know she's right.

She *will* forget later.

A Note from Madison

My mom quit drinking when she was taken to the hospital and learned how high her alcohol level was. We fought for a few more years and didn't resolve our problems until I was fourteen. I moved out a couple of times before coming back to her for good. We get along really well now and I wouldn't trade my mom for the world. She understands my humor and charm and the older I get I see where I get it from. I decided to write this story to untangle the web and to get my perspective across. Writing it has helped my mom and me understand each other's sides—why she was drinking, and why I was so mad for those two years. Writing also helped me get rid of my guilt. Our relationship affected my ninth-grade year because I had no one to motivate me. I ended that year with just .5 credit. Currently I am a junior at Scriber Lake High School and plan to either become a psychologist, an environmentalist, or a motivational speaker.

"But who's to blame? I guess we all change. We hurt the ones we love because of our pain." —Phora

HER

NIKOLAS COOK

There She is.

I see Her as I walk in a quick zig-zag through the spaces to lock up all the cars on the Subaru lot—my nightly, recurring routine.

Porter Robinson & Madeon's "Shelter" plays through my headphones as I stop and fix my eyes on Her: the blackish figure who has been with me for the past ten years. She is distant, farther away than usual, and She stares at me while pacing back and forth. As I try to figure out why, the rumbling sound of a boxer engine from a 2005 white STI roars past me on my left. She walks in a deliberate manner—as if She knows what is about to happen—in the direct path of the car. She continues to stare as She crosses her forearms to form an "X." I choke on the word "*Stop!*" as the car strikes Her with such force that She shatters like a pane of glass. Her body disintegrates and the pieces roll off the car and scatter on the ground.

Frantically, I look around to see if anyone is nearby, anyone who could have seen my reaction to what just happened. But I am completely alone. It's foggy with a light trickle of rain cooling the night, and spots of artificial light bounce off the cars. I feel cold, like an empty animal carcass, but I'm sweating as if I just ran a marathon.

That couldn't have just happened.

When I look again to see the pile of shards, they're gone.

Feeling numb, I begin to lock up again as the image replays like a GIF in my head.

Did She just commit suicide?

I try not to think about it, but I'm thrown back to the room where I had my first suicidal thought, on the day She appeared as my "friend" for the first time in second grade—in the classroom where I learned not to trust people and to withhold my emotions. The room that set the stage for the rest of my school career.

◈

I opened the faded salmon door to the well-lit hallway of the K-3 classrooms of Syre Elementary for my daily walk of shame—the one I'd been taking for a year. The march to the "special class," as my teachers liked to call it—the middle room with a window looking out to the dead, depressing courtyard. I made my way to the wooden desk in the back corner, as usual, where I was able to see everything in case I needed to escape from my social anxiety.

Richard walked over and sat down next to me wearing his usual reflective gold basketball shorts. He always wore Jordan apparel, like he lived in a gym.

"Hey," he said, loudly. I rolled my eyes. *Why did he always need to talk?*

"Hi," I answered, clenching my fist in agitation.

"You gonna read slow again and give up today?" he asked. He held back a smirk as he leaned in toward me.

I was caught off guard and unable to respond fast enough. *He stutters over every word,* I thought to myself. *I wish he could enjoy silence and leave me alone.*

"Hellooo?" he said. And then, "Maybe you should lighten up and stop being a bitch."

"Mhm," I muttered.

"I have a question for you."

"Cool," I answered as I glared at him.

"Why is it that you are so dumb? Maybe you should, like, stay in second grade." He squinted at me while he waited for my reaction.

My face grew hot and my mind started racing over different ways to react. *Who are you to say something like that? You're the same age as me and you have a low reading level, too,* I thought.

During the remaining forty minutes of class, I stared at the desk silently and felt uneasy in my stomach. At the beginning of first grade, my teacher had told me I read too slowly and that if I needed something, not to bother her about it. After that, when I had difficulty pronouncing words or stuttered over anything, the class would mimic me and laugh and she wouldn't do anything about it.

This humiliation was different, though. The person who was pointing out my flaws and making a mockery out of them was sitting right in front of me. I had been told that if someone makes fun of you, reacting just made it worse. But what was I to do? If I told on him I would be further ostracized.

When the bell rang and we lined up like ants to walk to the cafeteria, I was conscious of him walking behind me. We passed a half-dozen bright yellow signs with big black letters promising a "BULLY FREE ZONE." I wished those yellow signs would actually listen to my cries for help.

In the cafeteria everyone dispersed into their respective cliques, leaving me standing alone, listening to the voices bouncing off the walls. I felt overwhelmed. I dragged my body to the table where Richard sat. I hoped that killing him with kindness would actually work.

But he just picked up where he'd left off in the classroom.

"What are you doing here? No one wants to be around you," he said. He looked at his friends for back up—there were about ten of them surrounding him.

"Uhhh." I got up slowly, backed up and frantically looked for a new place to sit.

"Haha! Can you speak? Go away, you ugly faggot! No one likes you!"

"Yeah, go away!" the person next to him said, and then the rest of the table just stared at me and laughed as I walked away.

I dropped my lunch in the large black garbage bin and decided to head out to the field where the "neutral" kids always played kickball or soccer. They usually left me alone. Out on the field I went unnoticed for a few minutes until the popular kids showed up and decided to pick teams.

I was the only one left after everyone else had been chosen. I walked over to the team opposite of Richard's and made it halfway when he stepped out from the line and said, "No. You aren't gonna play with us. Take a hint and go away. There's a reason you didn't get chosen."

No one else said a word; they all looked at each other as if I didn't exist.

At that point I knew Richard's agenda to make me miserable would continue way past that day, which caused me to be on the edge of passing out while my stomach churned in anger. I felt that no one was there for me and no one ever would be.

Later, at home, I was losing myself in my mountain of Legos in the loft, trying to forget about the day while listening to the rain and wind whipping against the shingles on the roof. I smelled spaghetti being prepared in the kitchen when I heard footsteps on the stairs. My first thought was *Why is my mom coming up here?* She usually just yelled from downstairs that dinner was ready.

I felt a shiver, but I kept my head down and said, "Is dinner ready?"

No response.

"Hello?"

Silence.

When I turned around I saw Her for the first time: a dark, grayish figure with a dress and long hair.

"Hello?"

Still no answer. I could hear the carpet scrape with each step as She walked toward me. She had bone structure but no face. I could feel Her looking at me even though She didn't have any eyes.

"Um, what are you?"

I continued to attempt to communicate with Her, but She gave no response.

From that day on She was almost always with me when I was alone upstairs. It was an odd feeling to have my own "friend"—someone who never talked, yet who was always there. But as school got harder to deal with and I began to feel more empty and useless, She started to follow me in my normal, everyday life. She was the constant companion I always wanted but never had.

By the time I got to Einstein Middle, the figure was with me constantly. I wanted to kill myself almost every day. I was being called slow, retarded and dumb; my classmates made fun of my teeth, my size and how skinny I was. And even though we didn't have classes together anymore, Richard continued to find ways to bully me.

One day when he was walking with his group in the hallway, he stepped in front of me and asked his friends, "Who do you guys think would win in a fight, me or this faggot?"

"You, obviously," one of them taunted. "You'd be fighting a stick."

I had to stand there and take it. I knew they were right: I was dumb and annoying and useless.

I needed something to distract me from my suicidal thoughts, so I took it out on people who couldn't do anything back and on all the teachers who belittled me.

Every day I would walk into my general ed English class with a smirk and throw my bag into the air so it would land on my desk with a big *thump*. I would find the squeakiest chair, plop in it and rock. Then I would build my famous binder wall to create a barrier between me and the teachers for the war that was about to go down.

I would amp up the loudest people so the teachers had to fight to get us focused for the lesson. This battle usually took about ten minutes out of class, but of course I could keep it going by triggering someone with an insult or yelling something across the room.

"Alright class," the teacher would say three or four times, until her assistant, who was there to support all of the special ed kids, would finally step in with some muscle.

I heard "Nik, please sit down and be quiet" on a daily basis, which was just a signal that it was "on." I would fight her with smartass comments until the command changed to, "Nik, meet me outside."

During the hall discussions, the figure would mock the TA's gestures behind her back as I laughed and refused to respond.

The lectures always ended with me agreeing to go back to class without causing disruptions. I would return to my seat behind the barrier and think *fuck school*, then turn my game on high until I made the class erupt in a loud laugh and get escorted to the principal's office.

I had lunch detention every day, but I never went. I would throw away my lunch and hide on the field. I would go hungry the rest of the day, so eventually my body got used to it.

During this time She followed me around like a lost puppy. It was nice when I was home, but at school it was often annoying because She added to my stress and social anxiety; at school I couldn't deny that I was different. Every night I told my parents I had no homework—even though I had plenty—and played *Garry's Mod* on my PC to distance myself from reality. I would eat about half of my dinner, only to throw it up in the toilet an hour later. I could not make the figure go away, so eating was the only thing I felt I could control.

I would go to my room early to lie in the dark in my closet. She would stand right outside the door or sit on my bed, but wouldn't enter. Eventually I would leave the closet and lie down on my bed, bury my head in my pillow, and cry with Her right next to me. She would either look at the floor, look at me, or lie back on my bed.

One night I decided to end my life. I didn't have to explain why to Her because She already knew I thought I was nothing more than a waste of space.

Not wanting to leave a mess, I chose a clean, quiet method. I opened my door quietly and tiptoed out to the kitchen where I made a cocktail out of painkillers and cold medication—anything I could get my hands on—and stuffed them in my mouth. She was right there beside me, waving her arms, grabbing at my hands and trying to knock the bottles over. But I ignored her.

Instantly the back of my throat began to swell and all I could taste was salt, burning acid and the straight reality of wanting to die. I vomited out everything.

At Shorewood High School I found myself lying to cover the fact that I still had special ed classes, and I pretended to have a social life so people wouldn't assume I was a nobody. However, these things backfired and only made me more of a laughing stock. I ended up failing every class except Leadership and Choir—the only classes where I felt accepted—but even that ended. I was kicked out of Leadership for having bad grades, which did nothing but drill me deeper into depression, making me feel unaccomplished and useless. My only friend eventually got tired and wanted nothing to do with me.

This led to many more suicide attempts.

And She—She started acting differently. She would stay in the darkest places of my room, moping, always within eyesight, but disassociated from me.

During the spring of my sophomore year I was ready for my time at

Shoreline to be over. I wanted to leave a legacy—not to be remembered as the kid that nobody liked, but as the kid who went up on the roof and never came back. I had climbed up there three or four times before, after hours, and knew I needed to be up there one last time. I got someone to agree to take my picture from the ground to document it.

I ran and jumped on the steel downspout a few feet off the ground, and got my footing so I could grab the sharp ledge of the overhang. The hardest part was over. From there I pulled myself onto the roof and over the dividers, rolling over obstacles and running to the spot for my picture.

I leaned against the roof wall, feeling untouchable and free, watching the skyline. For those few seconds my heart slowed so much I could feel its intense thump on my toes as I realized I wasn't ever coming back.

She was with me, of course, in the silence.

"This is it. This is finally it," I said to Her. "After I get caught we are never coming back here. It's finally over." I felt weightless, knowing I would finally be free from all the pieces of shit I went to school with.

I stayed for a few minutes, then leapt back down just as the administrators came towards me like an army, as if I was about to shoot up the school.

That same night I attempted suicide again and was taken to the hospital. While staring at the white walls all I could think was *Why me?*

❧

Mechanically, I finish locking up the lots. As I walk back to the office I have vivid flashbacks of all the failed suicide attempts as well as the day She entered my life.

I miss Her.

Later that night I find myself in a dream: it's a warm summer day, and

I'm in my modern industrial house with a fantastic view. The wind picks up and a storm rolls over the snowy mountains. I try to go outside to see what is going on, but I get no more than two steps away from the door when it becomes a blank wall. I sprint to every door in the house, but the same thing happens. I pick up a chair and throw it as hard as I can at the window, but the second it touches the glass the window transforms into a blank wall of concrete. I try one last time, sprinting at the wall with all my strength. I smack into the concrete.

Finally, everything in my body tells me I can't fight any more.

I'll never be free.

I see a tombstone with my name on it outside the last window in the house: *suicide.*

I hear the grinding of concrete behind me, snap my head around to look toward the noise and watch a staircase sink into the ground: *drugs.*

A hatch door from above throws itself open and a ladder cascades down. I try climbing the ladder. I fall down half a dozen times, but I know this is the only way out: *coping.*

I wake up climbing.

It's time to let Her go.

A Note from Nik

This is my story for "The Movement." What's yours?

It's been about five months since She left my life that night at the car dealership. I had a horrible relapse with depression and lingering flashbacks afterward because I felt like a part of me was gone, but I know this transition has been for the best. I wrote this story to gain perspective about why I've been in the disciplinary track my entire school career, and to bring awareness to two issues: eating disorders among males and the stigma regarding schizophrenic tendencies. We are not people who sit in the corner talking to ourselves; we are functioning members of society, regardless of our medical issues. Schizophrenia needs to be talked about, and I encourage anyone who struggles with it to speak out. I know that it isn't easy to out yourself, because I avoided dealing with this part of me for years. I am currently trying to graduate, and next year I plan to go to Dirtfish Rally School in Snoqualmie to earn my Rally of America license so I can work for Subaru Rally Team USA and race stage rally. Dealing with my emotional issues is my number one priority, though, and I feel I am almost there.

I sold my own soul to the Devil
Said, "You don't need your heart"
In this world full of trouble
Where the madness won't stop
And they take advantage
And they run for the hills
'Cause a life is harder
When they swallow the pills
Being lonely

Took a walk with an angel
Because she said she can't fly
I screamed out, "Can you forgive me?"
Before she said goodbye
Well, go into darkness before I try
Is life worth living when you need to get by?
I'm still lonely

"Lonely" - Yoe Mase

BATTLE FOR BLUE RAIN BOOTS

HAILEY MORRIS

"Wait in the car. We're gonna surprise her," my mom says, nervously thumping on the steering wheel as we pull into the McDonald's parking lot.

When she gets out of the car, I fidget with my phone to keep myself busy, feeling the butterflies swarm in my already-jittery, coffee-filled stomach.

I watch from the window as my mom walks over to the CPS worker's car, opens the door and lifts Ali into her arms as he watches. Ali is wearing her bright blue rain boots and her long, blonde hair shines in the sun, making her almost glow. My heart drops when I see her face, smiling from ear to ear at my mom.

When they get back to our car, my mom opens the passenger door, points to me and says, "Ali, who's that?"

She gasps, and then, in her high-pitched, toddler voice, she says, "It's Sister!"

As I get out, she reaches for me and jumps into my arms, smiling. We hold each other tightly while the CPS worker and my mom talk in the background. I feel electric.

"I missed you," I say through tears. "I promised."

"Mhm..." she answers, still snuggling in.

It's been seven months since I've seen her, but that day is burned into my memory like it was yesterday.

❧

"Have Grandma drive as fast as she can," my mom said over the phone, her voice panicked.

"Wha...we're like um...five minutes away," I stuttered, but she had already hung up, leaving that sentence lingering in the air like smoke.

I was with my grandma and we were already on our way to my mom's for the weekend. I knew CPS was at her house to check up on the kids, but I didn't think much of it because that had been happening for a while. I figured she was just calling to see when I'd be home.

Something must have gone wrong.

Goose bumps traveled up and down my entire body.

It was such a beautiful summer day. We had the AC on, making Grandma's ocean breeze air freshener smell warm. Moments before I had been happily, obnoxiously serenading grandma with Bruno Mars' "Treasure." But suddenly it felt like we were in a cartoon scene where the grey clouds roll in and with one strike of lightning it's pouring down rain.

I chewed on the inside of my cheek for the remaining miles to my mom's old house on the hill.

The babies—Ali and Michael—weren't hers. Their real mom was my cousin, and she was a drug addict. When she brought Ali home my mom had fallen head over heels for her instantly, and had adopted her by the time we got Michael, Ali's brother, a year later. No one else would take him, and since we had Ali, she knew she couldn't separate them. She was so happy to finally have a baby boy in the house. We were a family of girls and he was such a sweet baby. He never fussed, only smiled and cooed. We had all become accustomed to the CPS visits; a law had been passed to check up on babies who had been born to drug-impacted mothers, but it hadn't taken effect until Michael was born. We had taken care of Ali while she was still going through withdrawals, and it was horrible. She cried for at least a month.

My mom lived in a duplex unit, and at first everything had gone well with the neighbor downstairs, a woman. But when the neighbor started dating an abusive man, a domestic violence call brought attention to the house. CPS was notified, and, because the kids were being monitored in that same space, they had been removed. Just like that.

We sped up the gravel driveway and I jumped out of the car as fast as I could to run up the stairs to our unit. The smell of baby wipes and coconut oil hit me as I flew past the two CPS workers who stood next to our beige couch with embroidered flowers.

Both Ali and Michael were in diapers, their hair mussed up because they had just woken up from a nap. Ali inhaled with excitement when she saw me. She ran into my arms and I kissed her all over her face.

"I love you. I love you," I said to her multiple times, terrified, feeling the blood draining from my face.

She just giggled and said, "You too."

Michael crawled into my lap and I held him with my other arm as he happily observed the people in the house. I kissed his forehead. "I love you, handsome," I said softly.

He smiled warmly and looked at me with doe eyes.

I was lightheaded and shaky, so it took everything I had to act strong for my mom while she talked to the CPS workers.

"Gather some things, like blankets or a stuffed animals, to make the babies feel more comfortable," my mom told me, so I put the kids on the couch to help her.

I felt my face get hot as resentment built toward the two women who stood in the living room, showing no emotion. My mom was repeating what they had just told her.

Will it really make them more comfortable to have a blanket from home where they should be instead of going to a stranger's home full of other kids they don't know?

A few minutes later the kids were hurried out the front door.

"Be good," I called after Ali, but she didn't respond. She knew she was going "bye bye" and was too excited to care where.

Tears began to well up and my voice disappeared. Ali focused on walking down the stairs while holding my mom's hand. "Can Sister come with?" she asked.

I broke, falling to my knees.

"No, Hailey has to stay here," my mom answered, calmly.

I wondered what she thought when she turned around to see me sitting on my knees, face bright red and eyes puffy. "I love you, Sister!" Ali yelled.

What could I do but yell back, my voice cracking? "I love you too, Baby!"

My mom shut the car door behind them and stepped away from the car. Her blonde hair was messy and thrown in a bun and she was wearing a t-shirt, leggings and fuzzy socks. Nap time clothes. My mom always napped when the kids did. I watched her cross her arms, shaking.

We waved goodbye to them through the car window.

Will we ever see them again?

We laid in the living room for the rest of the night, me on the couch and my mom in her chair. The house was dark, lit only by the stove light and the TV. Lifeless.

Out of all the people in the world, how could this happen to us?

I looked over at my mom, who just stared with glossy, blank eyes at the TV. I swear I heard my little brother cooing in his crib and my baby sister giggling. I stared out the window, questions cramming into my head like a huge weight.

Are they sound asleep? Terrified?

Do they miss us? Will they forget about us?

❧❧

When I put Ali down, she grabbed my hand and we walked together into McDonald's. It was surreal to me that I was actually holding her hand after all this time. I wished I could be holding Michael, too, but he had been adopted by the foster family and we no longer had legal rights to see him.

"Can I have some chicken nuggets?" Ali asked, as if I'd seen her yesterday.

When we sat down with our food in the cold playroom, it was empty. We were the only ones in the restaurant except for the occasional grab-and-go breakfast people. I wanted to ask her all the questions that came into my head, but it would have sounded like word vomit.

How is it with all of those kids around? Are they treating you well? Do you see Michael? Do you play together?

So all I could do was ask the basics.

"How are you?"

"Good," she answered between bites of chicken.

"Are you being good?"

"Yes."

Then she got a sly look on her face and poked me, like she always used to, and I played my part by dramatically claiming, "Oh no! That hurt!" making her giggle hysterically. This prompted more poking, laughing, and tickling. My mom sat across the table from us, glowing, so happy to see us together.

Two tables behind us, the keyboard clicked as the CPS worker with the curly bedhead took notes on everything. The whole time we ate and played in the big toy, he stayed far enough away to give us our "privacy," but his presence was a constant reminder that we would have to say goodbye.

After our two-hour visit, my mom started cleaning up the table and collecting Ali's things, I started to tingle all over, my stomach going in circles.

At the car, as I buckled Ali into her car seat, I choked back tears and said to the CPS worker, "Thank you for letting me come."

"You can come anytime," he answered, casually.

I kissed Ali one last time and said, "Be good."

"Don't cry," my mom said as we got into the car. "It's gonna be OK."

Even though I knew it wouldn't be, I chose to believe her because I needed to.

I put my sunglasses and headphones on and cried the whole way home, wishing my sweet baby sister was in the back seat singing to me.

A Note from Hailey

As of now, the kids are still in custody. Michael was adopted by the foster family, but we have visiting rights with Ali and my mom is still fighting for her. There were no stories in the other Scriber books about CPS wrongfully taking children from their homes, so even if it was the smallest voice, I wanted it to be heard. Just being able to tell so many people about what's dragging us down can be a weight lifted, and knowing that someone cares and hears us is all we really want. Writing our stories gives us the power to realize that although they might be terrible, they can never define who we truly are. Though some of us struggle longer than others, we still figure things out and eventually realize that we are able to write our own endings. As for my future, I'm working on graduating so I can go to school and become a nursing assistant for the elderly. Mostly, though, my focus is on getting my baby sister home safe with my mom and to be a family again.

ABSORBING THE DARK

JOCELYN CHAVEZ

"*Hello, Honey. Happy Valentine's Day. I hope you have a good time this wonderful day. I send a big hug and I love you.*"

The text from my dad comes at the beginning of P.E. At first I just stare at it and feel nothing. Then my vision blurs. I lock my phone and try to process what is happening.

Why now? If he can go four years without talking to me, why start now?

Tears fall on my glasses, so I take them off and try to clean them. Even though I don't want people to see me cry, my teacher notices. "Do you need to take a walk?" he asks.

I nod, get up, and walk into the hallway.

His text makes it seem like everything is fine, like everything I've been through doesn't matter. But he doesn't understand that I've always felt both his neglect and the effects of his actions very deeply.

When I was a baby my mom would cry to me and I would cry with her. She told me I knew exactly how she felt. When I was a few months old I started talking like a grown-up; my mom said I never used baby talk, only full sentences. On my first birthday I stood and started running. I didn't even walk first. My mom said I would make a pit stop for water and then start running again.

I feel like I've been running from the truth about my dad my whole life. I always wanted to think he was a good person, but I started to see the sad truth when I was four years old and living in California.

⚘

My aunt and uncle had just taken five of my cousins, my sister, my brother and me to the store. My mom stayed home because she needed to cook before my dad arrived.

When we came home my father was at the kitchen table eating with his brother, but we didn't see my mom. My uncle asked, "Where's Rosa?"

"She's in the room," he answered as he took a bite of rice and beans. His moustache hid his small upper lip as he chewed, and his beer gut was hidden under the table.

We all went to my parents' room and opened the door. The room was dark and she was slumped over at the edge of the bed, holding a tissue and crying.

"What happened?" my aunt asked, surprised.

"Adolfo hit me," my mom answered, her dark hair covering her face.

My dad yelled from the dining room with his deep voice, "No, I didn't! Stop lying."

Which one is lying? I wondered.

I was my dad's favorite and he always made sure I knew it. Whenever I cried he would hit whichever sibling was near and ask questions later, which made them hate me. My mom said that I was his favorite because I looked like him, and because I looked like him he could confirm I was his child. He was always accusing her of cheating. Just weeks before, we had celebrated my fourth birthday and Father's Day together because they fell on the same day. My mom made two cakes. One chocolate cake with strawberries for him and one vanilla princess cake for me.

Up until this point I thought everything was fine, but after seeing my mother cry silently on her bed, I questioned him for the first time. I realized, though, that this wasn't the first time something like this had happened.

Months before, I remember seeing my dad throw a plate at my mom when she had her back turned. This memory was disappearing almost like a bright light absorbing the dark. I could only see the still-frame strip, not the full movement of the scene. I could hear the audio, almost like the truth was starting to shine through.

"Why did you do that?" I remember asking him as he leaned against the sink.

"I didn't do anything."

"Yes, you did. I saw you."

"Because it didn't work anymore," he answered, just above a whisper. He stomped his heavy work boots as he walked angrily to the bedroom.

I followed him. "Why?"

He laid on the bed and didn't answer.

"Why?" I asked again.

"I'll just buy you new plates," he said, finally.

"Can they be green?"

He didn't answer my question. He just went to sleep.

Not long after this, one of our neighbors heard my dad yelling at my mom and called the police. He was arrested. That day I came back from school and asked where my dad was and my mom told me he was working late. The next day I went over to my cousin's house and he told me my dad had gone to jail. I didn't believe him, so I walked home and asked my mom if it was true. That's when I knew my dad had been arrested for domestic violence. Soon after, he was deported to Mexico.

For the next few years he was in and out of prison in Mexico. When he was out, he would cross the border and come back into our lives for short periods. His absence calmed my mom, which made things better. But I got in trouble for everything because my siblings and my mom took out their anger on me. When I was eight years old my mom moved us to Seattle and I didn't see him for four years.

When I was twelve my dad picked me up from my aunt's house during a visit from Seattle. His clothes were scattered on the floor of his beige van and the cloth roof was sliced. We stopped at a gas station to get some food for the night, then arrived at his house in Modesto. I had never seen it before. There was an apple tree in the front yard and a barn next to it. As we put away the groceries I wondered, *Why is his bed in the living room?*

I discovered the answer when he gave me a tour: his house was filled with cannabis. Every room had a different station for growing, dehydrating, fabricating, and selling.

I always heard my dad and uncle talking about going into the desert, and for the first time I realized what they meant...they had been growing it there until he started doing it out of his home. I also realized I'd seen him make a deal a few weeks before, but I was just beginning to put the pieces together.

I was at my aunt and uncle's house, late at night, looking for my dad. I hated being at their house because there were always a ton of people just hanging around. They were people who didn't have anywhere else to stay, but had money to spend for gambling. They would stay all day and all night.

The floor of the house was made up of cracks and dirt. A bunch of chickens, dogs, and cats roamed around inside the fenced yard.

I walked out to the volleyball court where people were making bets or buying candy or fruit with chili powder, but I didn't see him until I started back to the house. He was sitting in the passenger seat of a white truck talking to another man. He didn't notice me because they were both looking down.

As I walked closer to the truck he looked up, saw me, and motioned with a wave of his hand for me to go back into the house.

He looked rushed. I watched as they exchanged something, but I couldn't see what it was since the truck door was blocking my view.

What is he doing?

Then it hit me. I knew what was happening. I had seen drug transactions in movies. I also knew that when my dad went to "work" at night that he was going to the desert. I kind of knew he was a dealer, but I had never seen him in an exchange. His cover job was as a construction worker.

That's fucking great.

I walked back to the house and fell asleep outside on a couch with my cousin.

I felt helpless, like I could have done something to stop it if I had known earlier. I could have kept him from getting near my mom, pushed him away from drugs, yelled at him. I could have convinced him not to do any of those things.

When I was younger I liked to tell people he was rich. He did have a lot of money, but he never spent it on us. I knew what he was doing, but I didn't want to accept it. I wanted him to be a normal, good dad—a dad who had a normal job, something that wouldn't get him in trouble and deported from the country. I wanted him to have a normal house. I wanted him to get his papers so he could become a citizen and work for good things. I thought he was being deported because of citizenship issues. That was easier to believe.

I get to the bathroom and grab a paper towel to dab away the tears, then wipe trails of mascara from under my eyes.

I bet he doesn't know he just ruined $30 mascara.

He probably doesn't know how much I love makeup, how much I love to draw, or what my favorite color is. He probably doesn't know that I wear glasses or what kind of music I like. He probably doesn't know that my family always blames me for everything. He probably doesn't know that I have depression and anxiety and that when I say "I'm okay," I'm lying.

I take out my phone again and decide to reply.

"Thanks dad. I hope you have a good day, too. I love you, too."

A Note from Jocelyn

I haven't been in contact with my father since Valentine's Day. There's a high chance he'll forget my next birthday and message me a couple days later like he always does. I sometimes wish he was still in my life, but that he was a different dad who supported his family, or one who did anything for his kids instead of just trying to take us away from our mom to hurt her. I want him to be a dad who doesn't drink every day and who actually knows my hopes and dreams. I'm grateful to have a supportive mom who does everything for us. I decided to write my story because I know there are a lot of people in similar situations. I want them to feel comfortable to speak up and to try to get help before it's too late. Writing this has helped me realize how messed up everything really was, so it was like putting together the huge puzzle of my life. I understand better how my mom felt through all of it, and how she was finally strong enough to divorce him. I plan to go to college and get a degree in psychology so I can help others know that when you love a toxic person, you need to move away to have a better life.

Domestic violence hotline: 1-800-700-7233 or 1-800-787-3224

"FAMILY"

JOSH KIM

I can smell the weed and cigarettes from the elevator, down the hall from her apartment. When my mother opens the door, the first thing I notice is the weight she's lost since I last saw her two and a half years ago. She's gone from pear-shaped to stick-bug.

From all the drugs she's been doing.

She looks at me. "Oh, hi," she murmurs, then turns and walks back to the kitchen table.

I enter, looking around the small space. The bedroom door is cracked open enough for me to see a man lying on a bed—Chris, my mom's boyfriend. The thought of her moving on so quickly from her husband of twenty-eight years stirs up a pit of uncontrollable anger.

I place my backpack down on a small, round table next to a couch that's been made into a bed. "Can I have a cigarette?" I ask.

Without hesitating she scavenges through her purse, holds out a cigarette and slurs, "Here." She throws a wrinkled up $20 bill on the table. I reach down to pick it up.

She's giving me back the money she stole from me.

I swallow my anger and try again. "So how've you been?" I say, taking deep, slow breaths to calm myself down.

But it's terrifying to watch her because she can't hold still. She rocks back and forth, tapping her hands and feet uncontrollably. As she rambles, I notice that her hair is falling out and changing colors. I also realize that she doesn't care about me; she only cares about her next dose, her next bottle, and how she might be able to pawn something for money again, like the last time we were a whole family.

❦

"Get the fuck out of my house!" I heard my dad roar at my mother when I walked in the door, just home from my first day of eighth grade.

I made my way up the stairs and into my room, then threw my backpack down next to my nightstand. Looking around the corner into my parents' room I see my dad holding out his hands defensively, and my mom slouching, her back to the door.

Why do they always have to argue?

My parents would usually fight about something *I* did, like when they got a call from the school saying that I didn't turn my homework in on time, or that I missed a class or was getting bad grades.

But this fight was fierce, and it wasn't about me.

I went to my room and turned on some music, but I could still hear them yelling. By the tone of my dad's voice as he yelled "What the fuck?" and "Why me?", I knew she had done something to betray him.

"Get the fuck out! Get the fuck out! Get the fuck out!" he screamed louder, as if she hadn't been listening to him before. A few moments later, I saw my mom's clothes and purses fly out of their room into the hallway and down the stairs.

It felt like someone was tearing my soul in half. *Is this really happening right now? Why is my dad doing this? Is he really kicking Mom out?*

"Why are you doing this?! We can work things out, Dear!" my mom screamed in terror, calling out the name she used as her trump card with him to try to lighten the mood. But my dad continued to toss her stuff out of the room, stomping his feet so loudly the walls vibrated.

When I heard my mom leave our house that day I could not stop crying. She was my world. I loved her. For more than a year there was an ache in the pit of my stomach. But that feeling changed on my sixteenth birthday.

My dad had promised to take me out to help me buy my first car. However, at the bank, when we asked about my savings account, the lady at the desk told me, "You have no funds in your account, sir."

At that moment I knew my mother had taken my life savings, all $3,000; my parents were the only two who had access to it. And I was pretty sure she was using it for drugs. She didn't have a car, so what else would she use it for?

Frozen with heartache, I stood, speechless.

I didn't consider her my mother after that, let alone family. *A mother wouldn't steal money from her son.*

I started searching for something, anything, to fill the hole my mom had dug in my soul. I tried weed, oxy, triple C's, and alcohol, but nothing seemed to fill it. I went numb. I felt no love, no pain, no fear. Nothing. I was a blank person, someone who didn't mean anything to anyone.

My mom is mumbling under her breath; I can hear, but can't understand. As I smoke my cigarette I watch her and wonder if she's been wearing her nightgown all day. While staring at the mustard walls my mind runs through every possible solution to the problem of spending the night in this place.

I can't go back to my dad's. The beating he gave me hours before wasn't the worst beating physically, but it felt like the worst because I hadn't felt anything.

"I told you not to have the fucking school call me for anything," the text from

my dad read as I walked down 28th from school, just a few days after my thirteenth birthday.

I'd been having a pretty decent day until I got called out of my fourth period class to go to the principal. They wanted to talk to me about the scars my English teacher had noticed on my arm, but they made it seem like a "check-in." That's what they called it. They hadn't mentioned calling my dad about it so I figured the text I got from him was about my attendance.

I knew he would beat me for whatever it was. My heart dropped to my stomach and I felt short of breath, nervous and anxious at the same time. He didn't understand that he was one of the reasons I was hurting myself.

He hadn't been ready to be a father when my older brother was born, and he didn't step up when I was born, either. He maintained the household, but we never spent time together like a typical family; we didn't have dinner together or do things together, like go to fairs or movies.

When I got older he started beating me for being late to class or for being punished with lunch detention. He hated getting calls from school. The abuse escalated as time went on. Sometimes he would yell at me and break everything in my room, and sometimes he would go days without saying a word to me.

Knowing what was coming, I went to my room and lay down on my bed to wait for him. I stared at the ceiling with my lights off while listening to "Bullet" by Hollywood Undead, eventually drifting off to sleep.

I woke up to a kick to my bed. I jumped up, turned and looked at him standing next to me.

He gave me his *Are you ready?* look, then wrapped his hands around my throat and pushed me up against the wall. His third degree black belt in Taekwondo made up for the six inches I had on him; plus he knew how to get to me—it was more intimidation than strength. He held onto my throat, staring at me with piercing, dark brown eyes.

Then he punched me, his right fist to my left cheek, right below my eye. I just stared at him. I didn't feel anything.

With one hand he ripped my speakers from the power cord and whipped me a few times, then threw the cord at my T.V., shattering it.

"Why can't you just listen to me and follow my rules? What the fuck, Josh!" he growled.

Still frozen like a statue, I watched him yank my lamp off my nightstand. I put my arm up to protect my face right as he swung it toward me, smashing the light bulb on my forearm.

With no other objects close by, he hit me with his fist and open hand. Then he kicked my lower back—right above my tailbone—so hard I gasped.

"Maybe if you stopped doing stupid shit I wouldn't have to do this to you," he sneered.

I didn't feel anything during this beating. I was numb to it all.

Later that night, he told me, "Grab some clothes, you're staying with your mom for a while."

My throat throbbed. I was frozen. I couldn't believe the words that had just come out of his mouth. But maybe he was right.

Maybe I'd be better off at my mom's. She's never hit me before, and she doesn't care what I do.

I can't stand being with my mom another minute. Looking at her thinning hair and listening to her whining voice makes me aware of what's left inside me: an endless black pit.

Would I make everyone happy if I just disappear?

I decide my best option is to walk to my friend's house a few hours away. I grab my lighter, cell phone charger, headphones, and a small blade for cutting—everything I can fit into my pockets because a backpack would slow me down—and head out the door as she watches without emotion.

I think about calling the police or telling anyone that will listen about the abuse I'm dealing with. Then I remember: *Nobody cares about me.*

I've been by myself since the beginning, and I know I'll only get out of it alone. No one can help me with what I'm going through.

As I walk down the street I'm aware that everyone is looking at me and thinking, O*h he's just a nobody.*

A Note from Josh

I made it to my friend's house a few hours later, safe and exhausted. I was there for three hours before my dad found out I wasn't with my mom. I ended up going back to his house, only because my step-mom told both my brother and dad that if either one of them laid a finger on me she would call the cops and leave my dad. Things are going a lot better now. My step-mom made my dad realize that there were better ways to express himself and teach his kids than through physical abuse. My dad didn't grow up with a father figure; he went to military school back in Korea and his parents would beat him if he stepped out of line. Knowing his history helped me understand him better. As for my mom, I have completely cut ties with her. I decided to write this story to explain all the difficulties I've experienced, with and without help. I am proud of myself for writing it because I have always hidden everything from everyone. After not being open about anything in my personal life for so long, it feels like a big burden has now been lifted off of my shoulders just putting it all out there for everyone to know. I have been offered a few opportunities to go to colleges to study ballistics after I graduate. I came to Scriber with four credits, and with hard work, dedication, and hope, I managed to make up for my mistakes and catch up within two years. I believe that if you put your mind to it, it doesn't matter what other people say as long as you believe in yourself. Don't let others bring you down and tear you to pieces because of your mistakes. We're all human, we live and we learn.

"It's funny, cause I don't think they know what love really is, cause love ain't when you hurt a person, love ain't avoiding the problem you should be getting involved, love ain't when you pick somebody up by the neck then you grab his head and you slam it right into the wall." —Phora

THIS IS HOW FLOWERS GROW

KYRA WASBREKKE

"Good luck," my mom mumbles to my dad.

I can't see behind her sunglasses, but we avoid even indirect eye contact while they pack my bags into the bed of his truck.

Standing in the shadow of a grocery store, this transfer is taking place in a parking lot a few miles outside of Spokane. After a week of not knowing what was going to happen—after a week of anxiety-filled confusion—my dad is finally here.

The sun is shining and a light, cool breeze tumbles through the trees. I feel ten feet tall.

I climb into the back seat and throw my backpack on top of the pile of my dad's work clothes. I slam the door and hear the familiar sound of coins rattling and falling all over the floor from the side compartment. His car is always a mess.

"Hi, Mom," I say to my stepmom loudly enough for my mom to hear.

"Hey," she replies. She wears dark, purple-rimmed sunglasses and is casually scrolling through her phone.

The sound of my mom's trunk slamming makes me almost laugh; she does not approve of me calling anyone 'mom' but her, so the slam lets me know she heard it.

Just one week ago I believed I was never going to make it out of my mom's house alive. What happened between us changed my relationship with her forever, and I knew I could never, ever live with her again.

I settle into the drive back to Seattle, but I'm shaking at the memories.

≪⊱⊰≫

"This is what happens when your dad raises you," my mom said, gripping the steering wheel with both hands. She and my sister, Maaria, had just picked me up from school. Maaria was in the back seat on her phone and my mom was mad because I hadn't told my tennis coach that I would be missing practice. Every time I did something she didn't like she would bring it back to my dad, stepmom and their "poor parenting." And every time she mentioned him, it made me crazy.

"What does this have to do with my dad?" I snapped back.

Turning the corner, my mom hunched over the steering wheel, her body tense, and accelerated as we headed down the hill toward the house. She began to rant about all of my father's and step-mom's inadequacies: the way they let me get away with everything, how I was rude and selfish because of them.

"You're being a bitch!" I said, as condescendingly as possible.

While my mom's jealousy continued to unravel with increasing rants, I tried to remember the last time I felt like she was my real mom—when I used to love her as one. As long as I could remember she'd thrown parties for people much younger than she was. My sister and I were always surrounded by jello shots and slurred words, becoming aware of how a drunk person walked, talked, and acted at a very young age. Sometimes she'd ask me to sing or dance in front of her and her friends and I would go all out, doing anything that I could think of until everyone was howling in laughter. I thought it was normal to be drunk people's live entertainment. The older I got though, the more my resentment grew.

I wasn't sure how all of this had affected Maaria, but she never failed to take my mom's side on everything because of her resentment toward our dad. She continued to scroll through her phone silently as my mom yelled. But I was finally starting to accept that my mom was a shitty person, who would never change.

Keeping one hand on the steering wheel, my mom paused in her yelling, turned her angry face toward me, pulled her arm back and made a fist. She paused for a moment, then drove it right into my shoulder, hard enough to push me against the passenger door.

I felt a sharp sting from the impact of her knuckles and grabbed my arm in shock. I could feel steam bellowing from my toes all the way through my body and blowing out of my ears. "Don't touch me, you crazy bitch!" I screeched.

She exploded, making the car jerk and swivel from side to side as she screamed from her seat. She hit my arm again.

"Stay the fuck away from me!" I screamed.

Maaria joined in from the back seat. "Don't call her a bitch!"

"Fatass," I threw back, knowing it would hurt. She was very self-conscious about her weight.

Then we all started yelling so much I could barely tell who was saying what. But what came next I didn't expect. When the car stopped in front of our house, Maaria screamed, jumped into the front seat and began to slam her fist against my head so forcefully that all I saw was the blur of her bleached-blonde hair.

I curled up in the passenger seat with my head between my knees and just took the blows. She was so fast and forceful I couldn't count how many times she struck me. In my mind it felt silent even though the screaming continued. Cartoon-like blue and yellow stars stars danced in a melancholy groove in my vision. I felt like I was dying.

When she finally stopped hitting me, she got out of the car. She ran into the house, still screaming nonsense.

I snapped out of shock when my mom reached over me to grab my backpack. I realized she was trying to take all of my electronics so I wouldn't be able contact anyone for help. She had done this before.

In that moment I knew I was done with all the years of drinking, abuse, and manipulation. I hated her for living off every man she ever dated, for marrying a guy who left bruise marks on my legs in the shape of his hands.

I began to fight. I wasn't about to let her isolate me again.

We both grabbed the backpack straps and held onto them like we were in a tug-o-war. She pushed and scratched at me, then lifted up her her leg and kicked me in the chest and shoulder. I was getting squished into the passenger side window and could feel the door handle digging into my back. I pushed her with my shoulders and kicked her back. "You crazy bitch! You crazy bitch!" I screamed, over and over. All my life I had listened to her fight with boyfriends who called her the same thing.

After each of my screams she asked "Are you done?" Each time I responded with another opinion of her. My knuckles were white and my hands red and numb from holding onto the backpack.

She kept pulling my hair, kicking me and using her entire body to smother me.

For a moment I imagined how this must have looked to someone passing by: a grown woman pinning down and beating a fifteen year-old girl in the passenger seat of a fucked-up Ford on a cracked driveway.

My mom and I fought over that backpack for what seemed like an eternity. Every few minutes we would stop pulling and spit nasty words at each other. In the back of my mind I knew she was going to get the bag because I wasn't strong enough against her. My head was heavy and my body ached. I could feel each individual scratch, every fiber of me felt like it was swimming in hell. I finally gave up.

"You are not and never will be my mother!" I screamed.

When I got to my room, I saw my Nintendo 3DS sitting on my dresser—my only hope. The 3DS was able to connect to Facebook. I shoved it into the back of my pants. The only thought racing through my mind was if they took this, I would be completely trapped.

I heard my mom making her way into the house, her thundering footsteps headed straight toward my room. The pulse of my blood being pumped through my body made it seem like my heart had been placed right next to my ear drums, and it beat in insidious sync with my mom's footsteps.

When she and Maaria both showed up I began to trash my room. I scattered my makeup all over the dresser, pulled clothes out of drawers and threw them across the floor. I threw my art supplies and my drawings all over the place. Whatever makeup had fallen on the floor, Maaria started to grab at. As she shoved brushes and a compact mirror in her pockets, I pushed her away and we wrestled each other until my mom demanded that she leave. As soon as Maaria exited, my mom leaned against the doorframe with her phone in her hand, my dad on the other end.

"Come get me! They're crazy! Dad, they're going to kill me!" I yelled. She wouldn't let me speak to him, so I had to scream. I knew the only way I could get a message to him was to take this opportunity.

"Do you hear her?" she said to him. "This is the daughter you raised! Listen to how crazy she is. We didn't do anything to her."

I could hear his voice from the small speaker of her phone, but I couldn't clearly hear what he was saying.

Then she hung up, looked at me and said, "He's not coming to get you," mocking me like a bully. "You're stuck here with me forever. He's not gonna come and get you," she repeated, then laughed. Each individual 'ha' made me flare up more. I couldn't believe her, I didn't want to. If he didn't help, no one would.

She finally left me alone, surrounded by my lavender-colored walls. I sat on my twin mattress, which sat inside a queen-sized frame, and cried. My arms were numb and my head felt like it was going to burst. This wasn't supposed to happen anymore. I rested for only a moment before getting up to place my mattress, dresser and bed frame against my white door. I taped my blinds shut, and shut off my light.

I stopped for a moment to look at myself in the mirror. A fresh bruise was beginning to form on my right cheek, my blonde hair was frazzled, and my shirt was damp with sweat. My face was red and swollen from the screaming and crying. I looked like an Adonis flower.

I sat down on the bed again and listened to the blood rushing to my head. The constant drum in my ears made me feel like I was going crazy. I had always hated my mom's place, my room in particular. Her house never felt like home and my room never felt right. It felt dirty, even when it was clean, because everyone used it as a storage space. Old clothes and boxes filled with holiday crap were scattered everywhere so I had barely any room for my things.

One year earlier my mom had crossed a line in this room that made me decide I would never speak to her again. I only wished I had kept that promise. I had a friend over and we were playing games on my computer when my mom came in and yelled at us to be quiet. Angry with my response, she came over and grabbed long tufts of my hair and held up half of my body with it. The strands being pulled from my scalp felt like fire. Using my arms for support, I tried to push myself up to stop the intense pain. I let out a tiny yelp before she finally left, slamming the door behind her. I didn't say anything to my friend; I was used to my mom's abuse when I was alone, but this was the first time she had done something physical to me in front of a non-family member. My friend didn't say anything to me about it, either.

"I'm gonna get out of here. I'm gonna get out of here. I'm gonna get out of here," I chanted to myself as I rocked back and forth.

I knew I had to wait for the right moment to use my 3DS to get in contact with my friends because my mom had my Kindle and would be able to see any messages I sent on social media. For a while I just sat on my mattress, shaking, all kinds of thoughts going through my head. I was crying hysterically but I couldn't hear myself because of the ringing in my ears.

How long would it take me to walk from Spokane to Seattle? Should I call the police? Will they even believe me? Should I take pictures of the bruises forming on my head? If I sleep, they could easily kill me.

As despair took over, my chant changed to "Find something something *something* sharp." I was a year clean from cutting and I was incredibly proud of myself, but for the moment it was my only saving grace. My mind was buzzing. I knew I didn't want to do it, but in so many ways I felt I deserved it. I looked around until I remembered the shattered mirror under my bed, all the way in the back corner.

Sucking in my stomach, I crawled under and reached out until my fingers brushed against a huge shard. I grabbed it, crawled back out and sat in the corner diagonal from the door and stared at how pretty it looked with the light reflecting off of it. Finally, I took the sharpest edge and pushed it against the skin on my left arm. I pulled as hard as I could. I lifted the shard and did it again, and again, until I lost track. Until I felt that I had punished myself enough. By the end of it, my left arm was covered from wrist to elbow with stinging wounds.

I pulled up a chat room my friends and I had, hesitated for a moment, then typed, *They're beating me.*

I asked one of my friends to reach out to my stepmom because my dad was at work. I had no doubt that once he knew what was happening he'd come for me.

About an hour later my mom was at the door, pushing it open as far as she could against my barricade. "Give me your 3DS! I know you have it. I saw your lying messages!" she screamed.

Pushing my feet against the dresser, shaking uncontrollably, I screamed back at her, "No! It's mine!"

My sister came to help her push. I became too exhausted to fight them both and before I knew it, my mom was in my room, grabbing at the device with her long nails. For a moment we played tug-of-war, but soon she had it and left me alone, surrounded by my lavender colored walls.

All of my hope disappeared.

I found a full bottle of Biotin vitamins that warned of the danger of overdosing and felt relief to have at least one other option. I went through all the trash on my floor until I saw my history notebook. I turned to a blank page in the back and started to write to my dad's family and my friends.

To my loved ones,

If fate truly exists, then maybe this is mine. I've been staring at the walls for a while and the answer is beginning to paint itself out. Over and over I hear all the voices of my past whisper about how horrible of a person I am and how much of a waste I'm becoming. When I look in the mirror I see the shell of a body with no genuine soul. I'm not the type to question the entirety of the universe, but I constantly question why I'm here, or why I'm alive at all. For a horrible person like me, I think I would be better off dead.

"What's up with her haircut? It doesn't look good," my dad says, snickering at his own comment.

He pulls out onto the road and the three of us begin to debrief everything. It feels so good just to talk and know they get it. Old school rap music plays in the background as we fly through the desert landscape.

It has taken me almost fifteen years to figure out who my real family is. My mom has been with so many men that I've always questioned if I'm really my dad's kid. I hope I'm his kid. Biologically she may be my mom, but she's never felt like blood. Because I have her genes, though, I sometimes believe that I'm destined to become her. I don't want to grow up to be someone who abuses kids or manipulates loved ones for personal gain.

"I'm not putting up with her abuse anymore. I won't go back there or speak to her ever again," I tell them.

"You're old enough," my dad says. 'You don't have to see her anymore. You don't even have to talk to her. I can't make you do that."

As we drive through the desert, farther and farther from her, I feel light, like I'm flying.

A Note from Kyra

Trauma affects all victims differently. For me the journey past it has been about rediscovering who I am through understanding who I was. Even now, two and a half years later, the memories of this time still bring back fear. But writing my words down, and putting my story out there, has made me stronger. More importantly, being able to face these experiences head-on has given me perspective. I crave life more than I ever have, and all of it has made me see the beauty in the littlest things that life offers. I'm currently finishing my junior year, and very focused on making a career in the arts because I find artistic expression to be the best way to connect with others' experiences and emotions. I hope that in the future I can create something that will bring other troubled people the peace of knowing they're not alone in this world. My advice to whomever may be reading this, and looking for answers to their own problems is to simply be kind. And to know this: no matter how insignificant you feel, or how misunderstood you may find yourself to be, that somebody, somewhere, already understands exactly what you're going through.

"As we advance in life it becomes more and more difficult, but in fighting the difficulties the inmost strength of the heart is developed." —Vincent Van Gogh

WHO WE ARE

Left to right: Nikolas Cook, Shalyn Ensz, Alesandra Martin, Madison Aguilar, Jayden Green, Kyra Wasbrekke, Caleb Stine, Jocelyn Chavez, Sara Zaru, Marjie Bowker, Dave Zwaschka, Jesus Arteaga, Cameron Lundstrom-Helke, Akasia Traynor, Hailey Morris, AR, Shanija Nesbitt, Abbey Beuck. Not pictured: Josh Kim and Cruz Garcia

Scriber Lake High School is in the Edmonds School District, located just north of Seattle. Our school is one of choice; some students come to Scriber as freshmen, some come seeking a second chance, and some land here for a last chance. We are a school of small classrooms and caring teachers who strive toward creative approaches to learning. Scriber is a family.

ACKNOWLEDGEMENTS

This student writing/publishing program would not be possible without the backing of the Edmonds School District. We are especially grateful for the support of Superintendent Kris McDuffy, Assistant Superintendent Patrick Murphy, and Scriber Principal Andrea Hillman. We want to send special thanks to George Murray and the Edmonds Kiwanis for their devotion over the past five years; they have listened to our stories, bought sets of books for other high schools, and treated us to many, many lunches. We are grateful to Bob Fuller and the Lynnwood Rotary for their tremendous scholarship support and for making so many community connections for us. The Edmonds Daybreakers have supported our partnership with Seattle Public Theater from the beginning, and Seattle Public Theater has continually provided the best theater people in the city, Samara Lerman and Tim Smith-Stewart. Special thanks to Haifa Allhussieni of Café Louvre in Edmonds for her gracious hosting of our book readings every year.

We are grateful for the continued generous support of our extended Scriber family. Thank you all for your commitment to making sure these stories are heard in our community and beyond.

Marjie Bowker has taught English and History somewhere in the world for the past twenty years: China, Norway, and Vietnam, in addition to her "regular" spot at Scriber. She is co-founder of Steep Stairs Press and is the author of *Creating a Success Culture: Transforming Our Schools One Question at a Time* and two curriculum guides: *They Absolutely Want to Write: Teaching the Heart and Soul of Narrative Writing* and *Hippie Boy Teaching Guide: Transforming Lives Through Personal Storytelling*.

Shalyn Ensz is a Scriber graduate who learned how to use an Oxford comma before she learned to walk. Since joining the writing program she has been Student of the Month, Edmonds Rotary Daybreakers' Hidden Winner, and Lynnwood Rotary's Youth Challenge Award nominee and winner, among other academic acknowledgments. Before and after her early graduation, she has participated in and led dozens of speaking events beyond the Edmonds community and has been recognized by multiple newspapers and magazines for her work in both this year's and last year's Steep Stairs Press books. She hopes to become a fiction novelist as well as follow Marjie's footsteps teaching English in Norway

David Zwaschka has taught English over the last 25 years in Alaska, Tennessee, North Carolina, and Washington, with moments of administration between. His three years at Scriber have been a revelation; he has enjoyed his work with the school's terrific students and dedicated staff. Dave enjoys running, reading, hiking in the North Cascades, and not having any pets. He and his wife, Claire, have two daughters.

*Most of the basic material a writer works with
is acquired before the age of fifteen.*

—Willa Cather